Translator: Andrew Pastwood

This edition first published in 1993 by
The Promotional Reprint Company Limited,
produced exclusively for Fraser Stewart
Book Wholesale Ltd, Abbey Chambers, 4 Highbridge St
Waltham Abbey, Essex EN9 1DQ

Copyright © Editorial LIBSA, Narciso Serra, 25 – Tel 433 54 07 –
28007 MADRID
4.ª EDICION 1991
Copyright English language text © 1993 Promotional Reprint
Company Limited

ISBN 1 85648 138 7

Printed and bound in China.

ITALIAN COOKING

CONTENTS

INTRODUCTION

To be truthful, there is no such thing as 'Italian' cooking, for each region of the country rightly prides itself on its own culinary specialities. Nevertheless, there is a unique Italian quality to all these dishes. This derives partly from the freshness of the ingredients, partly from a style of cooking that is designed to enhance rather than disguise the flavour of it constituents and partly from a special Italian magic which captures the sparkle and liveliness of this sun-kissed Mediterranean country.

For many non-Italians, pasta epitomizes Italian cuisine and certainly there is a vast range of shapes and sizes. Yet even the extent to which pasta is cooked varies from region to region, let alone the vast array of sauces with which it is dressed. What a cook in Milan thinks of as al dente, that is cooked but still firm to the bite, a Neapolitan would consider soggy and overcooked! One rule, however, applies throughout the country: the pasta should be drained as soon as it is ready - not too thoroughly - and dressed immediately in whatever sauce you have chosen to use.

But pasta is only part of the story. Fresh fish, vegetables, fruit and herbs give Italian cooking its unique flavour - not forgetting that essential ingredient, olive oil. It is worth investing in a bottle of best-quality extra virgin olive oil for use in salad dressings and when grilling fish, for example. Outside its native country, it is rather too expensive to use for frying, except on special occasions; other vegetable oils, such as corn or sunflower, may be substituted, although they will not have the same characteristic flavour. Even olive oil varies from region to region, with Liguria, Apulia and Chianti each claiming to produce the best.

In the north of Italy, where olives do not grow, butter has been the traditional medium for frying, although even northern cooks are tending to use olive oil these days. Italian butter is always unsalted and margarine is really no substitute.

The traditional Italian meal consists of two courses of equal importance, rather than a smaller starter followed by a more substantial main course. Risotto or pasta are usually served as the first course of a lunch-time meal, while soup is more typically served at dinner. Meat or fish usually follows, although the former is not so widely eaten in Italy as it is in northern Europe and the United states. A vegetable or salad is usually served as an accompaniment. Fruit is the commonest dessert - and what could be more delicious than sun-warmed figs or freshly picked grapes. Pastries and puddings are usually prepared only for special occasions and formal entertaining

The recipes that follow include many lesser known specialities of Italy as well as some of world-famous traditional dishes, such as osso buco, zabaglione and risi e bisi. Feel free to explore and experiment, but remember that the freshest possible ingredients and a simplicity of touch are the key to Italian cooking.

ANTIPASTI

In Italian cooking, antipasti are more than simply starters or hors d'oeuvres. They are dishes served as a first course, whose purpose it is to get the gastric juices flowing with their aromatic or spicy flavours. In order only to whet the appetite and not to overwhelm it, these dishes have to bring together a number of qualities. They must be prepared with light, delicate and appetizing ingredients, which are easily digested and attractively presented. Their flavour must be subtle and not thirst-making. Neither should they be too sharp, bitter or spicy, as this would only detract from the main courses to follow.

Antipasti can be served in two ways: to the diners once they are seated at the table or laid out on a buffet table (perhaps in another room) and the diners may then help themselves.

Antipasti may be hot or cold and there are infinite possibilities. Among those served cold are various preparations of anchovies, herrings, caviar, mussels, cucumbers, prawns, oysters and all the other shellfish, ham, sausages, eggs, tartlets with a vast range of fillings, and smoked fish. In fact the list is virtually endless and limited only by the chef's imagination.

Hot antipasti, particularly fried dishes, are generally served after soup, as an introduction to the main course. These, too, must be lightly and delicately flavoured. They are not served when cold antipasti are featured on the menu. Hot antipasti include tartlets, vol-au-vents, patties and canapés. These are usually prepared with cheese and soufflé mixtures, fish and shellfish, liver, kidney and heart in a variety of sauces.

POTATO CAKES WITH MOZZARELLA

Serves 6

500 g/1 lb 2 oz potatoes, peeled
3 tbsp butter
salt
freshly ground black pepper
pinch nutmeg
1 egg, lightly beaten

1 tbsp grated Parmesan cheese
150 g/5 oz Mozzarella cheese, sliced

Boil the potatoes in salted water for 20 minutes or until cooked.

Preheat the oven to 220° C/ 425° F, gas mark 7. Grease an ovenproof tray with 2 tsp of the butter.

Drain the potatoes and return to low heat to dry. Add the remaining butter, salt, pepper and nutmeg and mash thoroughly.

Potato Cakes with Mozzarella

Remove the pan from the heat and add the egg and grated Parmesan cheese. Mix until thoroughly combined.

Place tablespoons of the cooled potato mixture on the prepared tray and pat them into the shape of biscuits. Place a slice of Mozzarella cheese on top of each potato cake. Bake for 10 minutes, until the melting cheese browns slightly. Serve immediately while piping hot.

SCAMPI BOATS

Serves 6

300 g/10 oz spinach
salt
30 g/1 oz butter
12 large cooked prawns or scampi, peeled and
   deveined
300 ml/10 fl oz Béchamel sauce (see Tomato
   Soufflé, below)
60 g/2 oz Parmesan cheese, grated
12 oval puff pastry boats

Preheat the oven to 220° C/425° F, gas mark 7.

Wash the spinach and cook in just the water clinging to its leaves for 8 minutes, or until tender. Drain thoroughly and chop coarsely. Season with a little salt and add the butter.

Prepare the Béchamel sauce and stir in half the grated Parmesan cheese. Place the pastry boats in an ovenproof baking dish. Put a layer of spinach into each pastry boat, and top with 2 prawns or scampi.

Pour the Béchamel sauce, which should be quite thick, over each boat and sprinkle over the remaining Parmesan cheese. Cook in the oven for 5-6 minutes, until the cheese and sauce have blended and turned golden.

NEAPOLITAN TOASTS

Serves 6

12 slices bread, 1 cm/1/2 inch thick, crusts
   removed
60 ml/2 fl oz olive oil
300 g/10 oz Mozzarella cheese, sliced
6 canned anchovies, halved
250 g/9 oz tomatoes, peeled, seeded and sliced
freshly ground black pepper
1/4 tsp dried oregano

Preheat the oven to 220° C/425° F, gas mark 7.

Cut the slices of bread in half. Heat half the oil in a frying-pan and fry the bread, on one side only, until golden. Add more oil if necessary.

Brush a baking sheet with a little of the remaining oil. Place the bread slices on the prepared baking sheet, golden side up. Put a slice of Mozzarella cheese, half an anchovy fillet and a slice of tomato on each toast. Season with pepper and oregano. Drizzle a little oil over each slice.

Cook in the oven for 10-12 minutes, or until the underside of the bread is cooked and the cheese has completely melted. Serve immediately while still hot.

MOZZARELLA IN TUNA SAUCE

Serves 6

1 tsp butter
60 g/2 oz dried mushrooms
2 tbsp vegetable oil
1 garlic clove
500 g/1 lb 2 oz tomatoes, skinned, seeded and
   roughly chopped
salt
120 g/4 oz canned tuna in oil, drained
500 g /1 lb 2 oz Mozzarella cheese
1 tbsp flour

Preheat the oven to 220° C/425° F, gas mark 7. Grease an ovenproof dish with the butter.

Soak the mushrooms in hot water, wash and rinse them thoroughly. Repeat this process several times.

Heat the oil and fry the garlic for 8-10 minutes, or until golden. Remove and discard the garlic.

Sieve the tomatoes and add to the pan, together with the mushrooms. Season with salt and simmer until the sauce has reduced substantially. Crumble in the tuna and cook for a few minutes more.

Cut the Mozzarella into 6-mm/1/4-inch thick slices and dust lightly with the flour. Arrange the slices in the prepared dish and place in the oven for 3-4 minutes, until the cheese has started to melt. Remove from the oven and pour the tuna sauce over the cheese. Serve immediately.

TOMATO SOUFFLÉ

Serves 6

150 g/5 oz plus 2 tsp butter
1 small onion, finely chopped
1 tbsp chopped basil
1 kg/2 1/4 lb tomatoes, skinned, seeded and
   chopped
salt
freshly ground black pepper
120 g/4 oz flour
600 ml/1 pint milk

60 g/2 oz Parmesan cheese, grated
60 g/2 oz Gruyère cheese, diced
4 eggs, separated

Preheat the oven to 180° C/350° F, gas mark 4. Grease a 900 ml/1 1/2 pint soufflé dish with 2 tsp of the butter.

Melt slightly less than half the remaining butter in a frying-pan, add the onion and basil and fry gently until golden. Add the tomatoes, season with the salt and pepper and cook until the mixture has reduced to a thick sauce.

Make a Béchamel sauce. Melt the remaining butter in a pan, stir in the flour and cook, stirring, for 2 minutes. Remove the pan from the heat and gradually stir in the milk. Return to the heat and simmer, stirring, for about 5 minutes. Remove from the heat, season with salt and pepper and add the Parmesan and Gruyère cheeses, reduced tomato sauce and egg yolks. Mix thoroughly.

Beat the egg whites until they form stiff peaks. Carefully fold into the mixture.

Pour the mixture into the prepared soufflé dish and level the surface. Cook in the oven for about 1 hour.

When the soufflé has risen and turned golden, remove from the oven and serve immediately.

GRILLED RADICCHIO

Serves 6

1.5 kg/3 1/4 lb radicchio
100 ml/3 1/2 fl oz olive oil
salt
freshly ground black pepper
170 g/6 oz Parmesan cheese, grated

Preheat the grill to medium and remove the rack from the pan.

Cut the radicchio into quarters and arrange in the grill pan. Pour over 90 ml/3 fl oz of the oil and season with salt and pepper. Grill for 10 minutes.

Transfer the radicchio to a warm serving dish, sprinkle over the Parmesan cheese and drizzle over the remaining oil.

Serve immediately the cheese has melted.

**Top: Pizzaiola Potatoes
(see page 50)
Bottom: Scampi Boats**

MINESTRA

From time immemorial, the *minestra* or soup has shared pride of place with various pasta dishes on the Italian family's dinner table. For example, for many years in Naples, the classic local dish was the *minestra maritata*, a thick fish soup. Recently, however, the Neapolitans have found fame with their incomparable preparation of macaroni.

The basis of minestra, as for all soups, is the stock. This is usually made with meat, although, occasionally, a vegetable stock is used instead.

Some form of starch is usually added to the basic stock to give it more body. For example, flour made from rice, wheat, oats or even pulses is added to the boiling stock, which should be stirred constantly to maintain smoothness and allowed to simmer for about 10 minutes.

There are many different stocks to be found in Italian cooking; we shall make use of the commonest.

CONSOMMÉ WITH PASSATELLI

Serves 6

2 tbsp flour, sifted
2 eggs
30 g/1 oz beef marrow

6 tbsp fine breadcrumbs
2 tbsp grated Parmesan cheese
salt
freshly ground black pepper
pinch nutmeg
2.5 litres/4¹/₂ pints chicken stock

First, make the pasta dough. Mix together the flour, eggs, marrow, breadcrumbs, Parmesan cheese, salt, pepper and nutmeg. Then knead thoroughly.

Bring the stock to the boil. Meanwhile, put the pasta through a mincer or passatelli maker, cutting the dough every 5 cm/ 2 inches with a knife and throwing it directly into the pan. Continue until all the passatelli are made and cooking. Lower the heat and allow to cook for about 5 minutes.

Serve immediately with extra grated Parmesan cheese handed separately.

Left: Consommé with Passatelli
Right: Roman-style Consommé with Capelletti (see page 12)

ROMAN-STYLE CONSOMMÉ WITH CAPELLETTI

Serves 6

Pasta:
500 g/1 lb 2 oz flour
4 eggs, beaten
2 tbsp water

Stuffing:
100 g/3¹/₂ oz tenderloin of pork
1 slice Mortadella
1 slice Parma ham
75 g/2¹/₂ oz chicken breast
60 g/2 oz lamb's brains
1 tbsp grated Parmesan cheese
1 egg
Marsala or sweet white wine
¹/₄ tsp nutmeg
salt
freshly ground black pepper
4 litres/7 pints clear stock

Garnish:
grated Parmesan cheese

To make the pasta dough, combine the flour, eggs and water in a mixing bowl and knead thoroughly. Add a little more water if the dough is not pliant. Set aside to rest for 30 minutes.

To make the stuffing, put all the ingredients in a food processor and blend well. Set aside in the refrigerator.

Roll out the dough thinly on a lightly floured board. Using a small wine glass or a pastry cutter, cut out circles 5 cm/ 2 inches in diameter. Place a teaspoonful of the stuffing on each dough circle, Brush the edges of the circles with a little water. Fold over the dough to form a half moon and press the edges firmly together to seal. Set aside on a lightly floured dish or board in a cool place for 24 hours.

To cook, bring the stock to the boil, add the cappelletti and simmer for about 20 minutes.

Serve immediately with grated Parmesan cheese handed separately.

VENETIAN BEAN AND TAGLIATELLE MINESTRA

Serves 6

500 g/1 lb 2 oz small haricot beans
250 g/9 oz belly of pork, roughly chopped
1 ham bone
2 tbsp vegetable oil
100 g/3¹/₂ oz streaky bacon, rinds removed and chopped
1 small onion, chopped
salt

freshly ground black pepper
1 tsp cinnamon
225 g/8 oz egg tagliatelle

Soak the beans in cold water overnight, or for at least 6 hours. Refresh with cold water, drain well and place in a large pan with the belly of pork and the ham bone.

Heat the oil and fry the bacon and onion for 6-8 minutes until just golden. Add to the beans, season with salt and pepper and sprinkle over the cinnamon. Add enough water to cover generously and cook, covered, over very low heat for at least 1 hour, or until the beans are cooked through.

Remove the ham bone and take off any meat. Cut the meat into small pieces and return to the pan.

If your tagliatelle is in the form of small nests, cut them in half. Otherwise, the tagliatelle should be in 15 cm/6 inch strands. Bring the minestra to the boil again, add salt and the tagliatelle. Simmer for about 12 minutes or until the pasta is *al dente*, cooked yet still firm.

Allow the minestra to rest for 2-3 minutes and then serve. This soup should be fairly thick.

CABBAGE MINESTRA ALLA MILANESE

Serves 6

1¹/₂ small green cabbages, quartered
salt
100 g/3¹/₂ oz belly of pork
250 g/9 oz Italian sausages
2 tbsp vegetable oil
1 medium onion, diced
1 small carrot, diced
1 celery stalk, diced
900 ml/1¹/₂ pints chicken stock
60 g/2 oz streaky bacon, rinds removed and diced
1 tbsp chopped parsley
2 tsp chopped sage
freshly ground black pepper
12 slices French bread
120 g/4 oz Parmesan cheese, grated

Trim the cabbage stalks. Boil the leaves in lightly salted water for 2-3 minutes. Drain, refresh with cold water and chop finely.

Boil the belly of pork and the sausages together for about 10 minutes. Drain and cut into 3-cm/1-inch pieces.

Heat the oil in a large pan, add the onion, carrot and celery and cook until soft and golden. Add the stock, and the bacon, parsley and sage. Increase the heat and when the stock starts to boil, add the cabbage. Season with salt and pepper and

cook for 8-10 minutes.

Toast the bread and place 2 slices in six individual soup plates. Pour over the minestra. Sprinkle with the Parmesan cheese to taste.

VEGETABLE STOCK

Makes about 1.5 litres/2¹/₂ pints

500 g/1 lb 2 oz potatoes, diced
2 medium onions, diced
1 medium head celery, diced
4 small carrots, diced
2 large tomatoes, diced
salt
freshly ground black pepper
1 clove

Place all the vegetables in a saucepan and cover with plenty of water. Season with salt and pepper and add the clove.

Bring to the boil, cover and simmer for 1¹/₂ hours. Drain the vegetables and set aside the liquid for use as stock.

CHICKEN STOCK

Makes about 2 litres/3¹/₂ pints

1 x 1 kg/2¹/₄ lb chicken★
3 carrots, chopped
1 onion, chopped
1 leek, chopped
3 celery stalks, chopped
1 tomato, sliced
1 bunch parsley
1 garlic clove, halved
1 bay leaf
2 cloves
salt

Put all the ingredients, except the salt, in a large saucepan and pour over just enough water to cover completely. Set the pan over medium heat and bring to the boil. Skim off any scum, reduce the heat to low and simmer for 1 hour.

Season with a little salt and simmer for a further 30 minutes.

Remove the chicken and strain the stock, which is now ready to use.

★ A boiling fowl is better than a roasting chicken, but less readily available. Allow an additional 1 hour for cooking if using a boiling fowl.

Top: Venetian Bean and Tagliatelle Minestra
Bottom: Cabbage Minestra alla Milanese

STRONG ITALIAN MEAT STOCK

Makes about 1.5 litres/2½ pints

2 dried mushrooms
100 g/3½ oz belly of pork, chopped
100 g/3½ oz streaky bacon, chopped
500 g/1¼ lb beef scrag
250 g/9 oz beef shin
salt
freshly ground black pepper
1 large onion, chopped
1 celery stalk, chopped
2 small carrots, chopped
1 garlic clove, chopped
1 bouquet garni
1 clove
60 ml/2 fl oz red wine
1 tbsp flour
1 tbsp tomato purée

Soak the mushrooms in warm water for 1 hour. Drain and wash thoroughly.

Preheat the oven to 190° C/375° F, gas mark 5.

Place the belly of pork and bacon in a large casserole. Season the beef scrag and beef shin with salt and pepper and place on top of the pork and bacon. Add the mushrooms, onion, celery, carrots, garlic and clove. Season with salt and pepper. Cover and cook in the oven for about 1 hour.

From time to time, check the casserole and give it a stir. When the meat begins to brown, add the bouquet garni and the wine. Return to the oven for a further 20 minutes to reduce the liquid.

Remove the casserole from the oven and add the flour, mixing it in well. Return to the oven for a few minutes before adding the tomato purée and enough water just to cover the meat. Stir thoroughly, add a little more salt and return to the oven for 4 hours.

Remove the casserole from the oven and take out the meat. Strain the liquid into a clean casserole and return to the oven, uncovered, for about 30 minutes. Allow the liquid to reduce to a fairly thick consistency, skimming off the fat when necessary. Strain the stock and keep in a cool place for up to 4 days.

The beef may be deglazed in the oven for 15 minutes, with a little of the stock, to make an excellent stew.

Note: Although it is important always to use good quality meat to make stock, you need not be wasteful. Italian cooks use many of the scrappy bones and pieces that would not normally be served as part of a meat dish. Indeed, the flavour of chicken stock is improved by the use of the head and feet as well as the body. Make sure that all feathers have been removed.

You can adapt the recipe for Chicken Stock on page 12 to make other stocks by substituting veal or beef for the chicken. You could also use half veal and half chicken wings. Lamb and pork are not suitable for making stock. You can also use almost any combination of vegetables.

It is important to avoid adding too much salt, as stocks are often reduced during the preparation of other dishes, which might then prove unpalatably salty. Do not add more than ½ tsp salt to 2 litres/3½ pints stock, preferably towards the end of the cooking time.

Top: Vegetable Stock (see page 12)
Bottom: Strong Italian Meat Stock

MINESTRONE

Minestrone may be thought of as being somewhere between the *minestra* and *pasta asciutta*. It is thicker than the former, although still a soup, while the latter has no liquid at all.

Minestrone is based on three principal ingredients: vegetables and/or pulses, herbs and fats. The fats usually used are pork fats, but during Lent, a time of gastronomic denial in Catholic countries, they are replaced by oil. The precise ingredients of minestrone vary from region to region. In Genoa, where it is thought to have originated, it is usually made with pumpkin, cabbage, beans, tomatoes and three types of pasta. In Milan, however, it is more typically made with rice. It is universally served with a separate dish of grated Parmesan cheese.

Minestrone is one of those dishes that improves on reheating. It can be stored in the refrigerator for up to three days, but it is not suitable for freezing.

TOMATO MINESTRONE WITH RICE AND CHICORY

Serves 6

1 tbsp vegetable oil
1 small onion, diced
100 g/3¹/₂ oz pork fat or streaky bacon, diced
1 garlic clove, crushed
1 tbsp chopped parsley
1 celery stalk, chopped
1 carrot, chopped
10 tomatoes, skinned, seeded and chopped
600 ml/1 pint water
1 kg/2¹/₄ lb chicory, chopped
salt
freshly ground black pepper
350 g/12 oz rice

Heat the oil in a flameproof casserole and sauté the onion. Add the pork fat or streaky bacon, garlic, parsley, celery and carrot and cook for 3-5 minutes. Add the tomatoes, and a little water if necessary to stop the mixture scorching.

Cook over low heat for 10 minutes. Add the chicory and cook for 5 minutes. Season with salt and pepper and add the remaining water.

Continue to cook for a further few minutes until the chicory is tender, then add the rice and simmer for about 15 minutes, or until the rice is cooked.

FLORENTINE MINESTRONE

Serves 6

100 ml/3¹/₂ fl oz oil
1 medium onion, chopped
1 garlic clove, crushed
170 g/6 oz fatty ham or streaky bacon, rinds removed and chopped
1 small red cabbage, chopped
1 leek, white only, chopped
1 celery stalk
500 g/1 lb 2 oz cooked small haricot beans
1 meaty ham bone
2 tbsp tomato purée
200-300 ml/7-10 fl oz stock
salt
freshly ground black pepper
6 slices dark bread, toasted

Soffritto:
100 ml/3¹/₂ fl oz vegetable oil
2 garlic cloves
2-3 rosemary sprigs

Heat a little of the oil in a flameproof casserole and sauté the chopped onion. Crush one of the garlic cloves and add to the casserole, together with the chopped ham or bacon. When the onions turn golden, add the red cabbage, leek and celery. Then add the cooked beans, ham bone and tomato purée.

Cook over low heat, stirring occasionally, until the vegetables begin to soften. Add a little stock, season with salt and pepper to taste, cover and cook gently for about 1 hour, adding more stock if necessary.

To make the *soffritto*, put the oil in a frying-pan and add the garlic cloves and the rosemary. Fry over high heat until the garlic turns golden brown. Pour this now scented oil into the minestrone through a strainer. Cook for a further 15 minutes, to allow it to absorb the oil.

Place the toasted bread in six individual soup bowls. Pour over the soup and serve immediately. Alternatively, add the toasted bread to the soup at the same time as the *soffritto* and allow to cook.

Note: The aromatic oil of the *soffritto* is what characterizes this minestrone from Florence.

Florentine Minestrone

POLENTA

Polenta is a typically Italian preparation which is made by boiling coarsely ground cornmeal (polenta flour) in salted water. It is a winter dish principally because polenta flour does not stay fresh in hot weather and it somehow suits colder weather.

Cooking polenta is very simple, but you must be careful to use exactly the right proportions of water to flour. The problem is that the rate of absorption varies from one batch of flour to another, so it is never possible to quantify exactly. As a rule of thumb, you will require 1.4 litres/2½ pints salted water and 500 g/1 lb 2 oz polenta flour for six servings.

To make the polenta, bring the salted water to the boil in a saucepan. Add the polenta flour by pouring it in slowly in a thin stream, stirring constantly with a wooden spoon. The polenta is cooked when it comes away easily from the sides of the pan, after about 30-40 minutes of simmering over medium heat.

When the polenta is cooked, turn it out on to a clean napkin spread over a wooden board. It may be served immediately as part of a dish or allowed to cool before further cooking.

POLENTA WITH MOZZARELLA AND ANCHOVIES

Serves 6

Polenta:
1.5 litres/2½ pints water
salt
500 g/1 lb 2 oz polenta flour
30 g/1 oz butter

Topping:
300 g/10 oz Mozzarella cheese, diced
75 g/2½ oz canned anchovies, rinsed
1 kg/2¼ lb tomatoes, peeled, seeded and chopped
freshly ground black pepper
3 tbsp vegetable oil

Prepare the polenta as above, so that it is fairly thick. Meanwhile, grease a cake tin with the butter. Remove the polenta from the heat and pour it into the prepared cake tin. Level off the polenta and set aside to cool.

Preheat the oven to 190° C/375° F, gas mark 5.

When the polenta is cold, sprinkle over the Mozzarella and anchovies. Spread the chopped tomatoes over the top and season with salt and pepper. Drizzle over the oil and cook in the oven for 15 minutes.

POLENTA WITH SPARE RIBS

Serves 6

150 g/5 oz belly of pork
1 medium onion
1 carrot
1 celery stalk
parsley sprigs
3 tbsp olive oil
1 kg/2¼ lb pork spare ribs, chopped in half
1 large can tomatoes
salt
225-450 ml/8-16 fl oz water
60 g/2 oz Parmesan cheese, grated

Polenta:
1.5 litres/2½ pints water
500 g/1 lb 2 oz polenta flour
salt
30 g/1 oz butter

Top: Polenta with Spare Ribs
Bottom: Polenta with Mozzarella and Anchovies

Prepare the polenta as above. Grease a cake tin or individual dariole moulds with the butter. Pour in the polenta and keep warm.

Put the belly of pork, onion, carrot, celery and parsley into a blender and reduce to a coarse paste.

Heat the oil in a flameproof casserole, add the paste and fry gently for a few minutes. Add the spare ribs and fry for several minutes before adding the tomatoes, salt and water. Cover and cook over low heat for at least 1 hour.

When the meat on the ribs is almost coming off the bones and the juices have thickened, remove from the heat and take out the spare ribs. Strip the meat off the bones and cut it into small pieces. Return the meat to the casserole.

Serve the meat straight from the casserole with the warm polenta, garnished with parsley sprigs and small pieces of braised celery, if liked. Sprinkle over a little grated Parmesan cheese and serve the remainder separately.

ZUPPE

Zuppe are not exactly soups, although they are semi-liquid and usually served with slices of toasted bread. They are made with a wide variety of ingredients, often including a base of meat stock, butter and *pesto*. (The main ingredients of *pesto* are basil, pine nuts, olive oil and garlic.)

That's the theory, but in practice there are variations. During Lent, abstaining from meat means that the meat stock is replaced by one made from vegetables.

ZUPPA OF BEANS AND SPINACH

Serves 6

400 g/14 oz small haricot beans
1 tbsp flour
1 kg/2¼ lb spinach
1 tbsp oil
1 small onion, diced
1 carrot, diced
1 celery stalk, diced
120 g/4 oz streaky bacon, rinds removed and diced
1 garlic clove, crushed
1 tbsp chopped parsley
salt
freshly ground black pepper
12 slices French bread, toasted

Soak the beans overnight in cold water mixed with the flour. Drain and transfer them to a large flameproof casserole. Cover with fresh water and cook over low heat for about 1 hour until fairly soft.

Wash the spinach and cook in just the water clinging to the leaves for about 5 minutes. Drain thoroughly and chop finely.

Heat the oil in a large saucepan and fry the onion, carrot, celery, bacon, garlic and parsley until just golden. Add 2 tbsp water. Stir in the beans and the spinach and season with salt and pepper. Cook for a few minutes to allow the ingredients to blend together well, stirring thoroughly. Just before serving, add the toast to the zuppa and stir once carefully.

Top: Zuppa of Beans and Spinach
Bottom: Zuppa Acquacotta

ZUPPA ACQUACOTTA

Serves 6

1 kg/2¼ lb tomatoes, skinned and seeded
4 onions, sliced
1 tbsp chopped mint
salt
freshly ground black pepper
12 slices French bread
120 ml/4 fl oz olive oil
30 g/1 oz Parmesan cheese, grated

Cook the tomatoes in very little water for a few minutes. Add the onion, mint and season with salt. Cover and cook over low heat for about 30 minutes, until the mixture becomes a thick sauce.

Meanwhile, arrange the slices of bread in a dish and pour the oil over them. Season with salt and pepper.

When the tomato mixture is ready, pour it, still boiling, over the bread and sprinkle liberally with the grated Parmesan cheese.

Note: *Acquacotta* literally means 'cooked water'. This dish may be found in various regions, but probably originated in Umbria.

POTATO ZUPPA

Serves 6

1 kg/2¹/₄ lb potatoes, peeled
salt
30 g/1 oz butter
1 small onion, diced
1 carrot, diced
1 celery stalk, diced
1 garlic clove, crushed
1 tbsp chopped parsley
freshly ground black pepper
75 ml/2¹/₂ fl oz milk

Garnish:
60 g/2 oz croûtons

Boil the potatoes in lightly salted water for 20-25 minutes or until cooked.

Drain and reserve the cooking liquid. Mash the potatoes and return them to the water in which they were cooked. Keep warm.

Melt the butter in a frying-pan and fry the onion, carrot, celery, garlic and parsley over low heat until golden. Season with salt and pepper and add to the potato purée. Stir thoroughly to mix and heat gently for a few minutes until thoroughly warmed. If the zuppa is too thick, thin it with a little milk.

Transfer the soup to a tureen, garnish with the fried croûtons and serve immediately.

Potato Zuppa

FAKE FISH ZUPPA

Serves 6

2 x 37 g/1¹/₂ oz cans anchovies
75 ml/2¹/₂ fl oz vegetable oil
2 garlic cloves, crushed
2 tbsp chopped parsley
2 tbsp tomato purée
salt
freshly ground black pepper
6 slices white bread
2.5 litres/4¹/₂ pints water
12 slices French bread

Drain the anchovies thoroughly. Soak them in warm water for a few minutes, drain and pat dry with absorbent kitchen paper towels.

Heat the oil in a heavy-based saucepan and fry the garlic until golden. Add the anchovies and half the parsley. Dilute the tomato purée with a little water and add to the pan. Season with salt and pepper and simmer gently.

Soak the white bread in the water for 15 minutes. When it has softened, squeeze out as much of the water as you can with your hands. Tip the bread pulp into a sieve and press with a wooden spoon to extract the remaining moisture.

Put the soaked bread into a mixing bowl. Stir in the tomato sauce, a little at a time, stirring constantly with a wooden spoon to keep the resultant thick mixture as smooth as possible.

Pour the mixture into the saucepan, little by little to retain the smoothness. It will continue to thicken. Allow to cook very gently for a few more minutes.

Meanwhile, toast the French bread, rubbing the slices on each side with garlic, if liked. Put half the slices into the simmering *zuppa*.

Pour the *zuppa* into a tureen and arrange the remaining French bread slices on top. Sprinkle over the remaining parsley just before serving.

Fake Fish Zuppa

PASTA

Pasta presents us with an almost infinite range of shapes and sizes which vary greatly from one region to another, so that it is almost impossible to classify it completely.

Pasta itself is based on a simple dough mixture. The variety in pasta dishes comes from the different shapes and sizes the dough is made into and, of course, the different ingredients with which the sauce and dishes are cooked.

An important distinction should be made between plain flat pasta, such as *tagliatelle, fettuccine, pappardelle* and *lasagna*, and the stuffed varieties, such as *tortellini, agnolotti, cappelletti, ravioli, cannelloni* and *tortelli*. The pasta may vary in the number of eggs used to make the dough and the consistency of the sheets.

There are also cylindrical and hollow pasta shapes. Among the former are *capelli*

d'angelo, capellini, vermicelli and *spaghetti*. The latter includes *zite, bucatini, perciatelli, candele* and, of course, *macaroni*.

Finally there is the infinite variety of small pasta and pasta for soups: *penne, mostaccioli, ditalini, conchiglie, gnocchi, linguine, stelline, anellini, farfalline* – and so on.

SPAGHETTI CON VONGOLE (PASTA WITH CLAMS)

Serves 6

1.5 kg/3¼ lb clams
90-120 ml/3-4 fl oz vegetable oil
1 clove garlic
1.5 kg/3¼ lb tomatoes, skinned, seeded, chopped and sieved
salt
freshly ground black pepper
1-2 tbsp chopped parsley
700 g/1½ lb spaghetti

Scrub the clams under cold running water. Discard any that do not shut immediately when sharply tapped.

Place the clams in a pan with a little of the oil, cover and set over fairly high heat for a few minutes, shaking the pan occasionally, until the clams have opened. Remove from the heat and set aside to cool.

Drain the clams and reserve the cooking liquid. Discard any clams that have not opened. Separate the flesh from the shells and pour warm water over the clams to remove any last traces of grit. Transfer them singly to another dish and set aside.

Strain the reserved cooking liquid through clean muslin or cheesecloth to remove all grit and sand. Pour the cooking liquid over the clams.

Heat the remaining oil in a large saucepan and fry the garlic until it turns golden. Remove and discard the garlic. Add the tomatoes to the oil and season with salt and pepper.

Strain the clams and reserve the cooking liquid. Set the clams aside. Add the clam

Left: Cannelloni Etruscan Style (see page 24)
Right top: Spaghetti Con Vongole
Right bottom: Macaroni with Aubergines (see page 24)

cooking liquid and a little water, if necessary, to the tomatoes and cook over the lowest possible heat for at least 1 hour.

When the sauce has reduced to a thick paste, add the clams and chopped parsley. Simmer for a few more minutes.

Meanwhile, cook the spaghetti in a large pan of boiling, lightly salted water until *al dente*, about 8-10 minutes. Remove the pan from the heat, drain and transfer the pasta to a serving bowl. Add the clam sauce, mix well and serve while still very hot.

PENNE SAN GIOVANNELLO

Serves 8

60 g/2 oz butter
60 g/2 oz lard
3 garlic cloves, chopped
150 g/5 oz streaky bacon, rinds removed and chopped
1.5 kg/3¼ lb canned tomatoes, drained and finely chopped
salt
freshly ground black pepper
800 g/1¾ lb penne
100 g/3½ oz Gruyère cheese, grated
1-2 tbsp chopped basil

Melt the butter and the lard in a large frying-pan over low heat. Gently fry the garlic and chopped bacon until the garlic begins to turn golden. Add the chopped tomatoes and season with salt and pepper.

Meanwhile, cook the penne in a large pan of boiling salted water until *al dente*, about 12-15 minutes.

Remove the pan from the heat, drain the pasta and add to the sauce in the frying-pan for 1-2 minutes. Transfer the pasta mixture to a heated serving dish, sprinkle over the grated cheese and chopped basil and serve immediately.

Note: Penne are not dissimilar to macaroni and are available from most branches of the large supermarket chains.

Left: Penne San Giovannello
Right: Calabrian Spaghetti
(see page 24)

CANNELLONI ETRUSCAN STYLE

Serves 6

Pasta:
150 g/5 oz flour
1 egg
1 egg yolk
salt
30 g/1 oz butter

Filling and sauce:
60 g/2 oz plus 1 tbsp butter
60 g/2 oz flour
400 ml/14 fl oz milk
60 g/2 oz Parmesan cheese, grated
300 g/10 oz mushrooms, sliced and softened
  in butter
75 g/2¹/₂ oz Gruyère cheese, diced
60 g/2 oz Parma ham, diced

To prepare the pasta dough, place the flour in a mixing bowl and make a well in the centre. Add the egg and the egg yolk and mix in thoroughly. Set aside to rest for about 30 minutes.

Roll out the dough into a square and, with the point of a knife, cut it into 8-cm/3-inch squares.

Bring a saucepan of lightly salted water to the boil and drop in the first pasta square very carefully. Cook until *al dente*, which should take no longer than 2-3 minutes. Take out the square and lay it on a slightly dampened tea cloth or napkin. Continue cooking all the squares in the same way.

To make the filling, first make a fairly thick Béchamel sauce as follows. Melt 60 g/2 oz of the butter in a pan, stir in the flour and cook, stirring, for 2-3 minutes. Remove from the heat and gradually stir in 300 ml/10 fl oz of the milk. Return to the heat and bring to the boil stirring. Reduce the heat and simmer, stirring, for about 5 minutes or until the sauce is thick and smooth.

Preheat the oven to 220°C/425°F, gas mark 7. Grease an ovenproof dish with the remaining butter.

Pour two-thirds of the Béchamel sauce into a mixing bowl and add half the Parmesan cheese and all the mushrooms. Season with salt.

Divide the mixture equally between the pasta squares, roll up and seal the edges. Arrange the cannelloni, seam side down, in the prepared ovenproof dish. Sprinkle over the diced Gruyère cheese and the Parma ham.

Heat the remaining Béchamel sauce with the remaining milk and stir vigorously over moderately high heat. Pour over the cannelloni and sprinkle over the remaining Parmesan cheese.

Bake for 15 minutes, or until the top has browned slightly. Serve immediately.

CALABRIAN SPAGHETTI

Serves 6

350 g/12 oz broccoli
salt
170 ml/6 fl oz vegetable oil
3 garlic cloves, chopped
1 kg/2¹/₄ lb canned tomatoes, drained and
  finely chopped
60 g/2 oz seedless raisins
60 g/2 oz pine kernels, dry roasted
700 g/1¹/₂ lb spaghetti
1 tbsp chopped parsley

Cook the broccoli in lightly salted boiling water for 12-15 minutes or until just tender. Drain and cut off the florets and keep warm.

Heat the oil in a frying-pan, add the chopped garlic and cook until it is beginning to turn golden. Add the chopped tomatoes and continue cooking for about 10 minutes, over moderate heat. Stir in the raisins and pine kernels.

Cook the spaghetti in lightly salted, boiling water for 8-10 minutes, or until *al dente*. (As the spaghetti softens, curl it around the inside of the pan so that it fits.)

Drain the spaghetti and transfer it to a warm serving dish. Arrange the broccoli florets on top and pour over the sauce. Finally, sprinkle with the parsley and serve immediately.

Note: This dish is known in Italy as Spaghetti Calabrese. *Calabrese* is, of course, the Italian word for broccoli as well as meaning 'from Calabria'.

MACARONI WITH AUBERGINES

Serves 6

150 g/5 oz butter
2 tbsp olive oil
1 medium onion, finely chopped
6 anchovy fillets
4 medium aubergines, peeled and diced
1.5 kg/3¹/₄ lb tomatoes, skinned, seeded and
  chopped
1 garlic clove, chopped
2 tbsp chopped parsley
salt
freshly ground black pepper
700 g/1¹/₂ lb macaroni
60 g/2 oz Gruyère cheese, grated
6 tbsp grated Parmesan cheese

Melt 60 g/2 oz of the butter with the oil in a large, heavy-based saucepan. Add the sliced onion, cover and cook over low heat to soften the onion.

Remove the pan from the heat, add the anchovies and mash them into the onions with a fork. Return to the heat and add the aubergines, tomatoes, garlic and parsley. Season with salt and pepper, mix well, cover and cook over low heat for 30 minutes. Stir occasionally and add a little warm water if the mixture becomes too thick or seems likely to scorch.

Cook the macaroni in vigorously boiling, salted water. When it is *al dente*, after about 12-15 minutes, drain and transfer to a warm serving dish. Pour over the aubergine sauce. Add the remaining butter and the Gruyère and Parmesan cheeses. Mix well and serve immediately.

FETTUCCINE PIEDMONT STYLE

Serves 6

Pasta :
500 g/18 oz flour
4 eggs, lightly beaten
1 tbsp olive oil
30 g/1 oz Parmesan cheese, grated
salt

Sauce :
75 g/2¹/₂ oz butter, diced
100g/3¹/₂ oz Parmesan cheese, grated
pinch nutmeg
freshly ground white pepper
1 white truffle
300 ml/10 fl oz strong Italian meat stock (see
  page 14)

To prepare the pasta, place the flour in a mixing bowl and make a well in the middle. Add the eggs, oil, Parmesan cheese and a little salt. Mix well and knead the dough, adding a little cold water if necessary. Set aside to rest for about 30 minutes.

Roll out the dough and cut into strips about 1 cm/¹/₂ inch wide.

Bring a pan of lightly salted water to the boil and cook the pasta for 8-10 minutes, until *al dente*.

Drain and place in a warm dish. Add the butter and half the Parmesan cheese and season with nutmeg and pepper. Stir well and divide between 6 individual plates. Shave a small quantity of the truffle over each. Serve immediately, handing the Italian meat stock and remaining Parmesan cheese separately.

LASAGNA ALLA MARCHESE

Serves 6

Pasta:
225 g/8 oz spinach
500 g/1 lb 2 oz flour, sifted
2 eggs, lightly beaten
salt
1 tbsp oil

Sauce:
500 ml/18 fl oz Bolognese sauce (homemade
  or canned)
30 g /1 oz plus 2 tsp butter
100 g/3½ oz cold cooked chicken, diced
120 g/4 oz grated Parmesan cheese
1 black truffle (optional)

Wash the spinach thoroughly and cook in just the water clinging to the leaves for several minutes. Remove from the heat and refresh under cold running water. Drain, chop coarsely sieve and set aside to cool.

To prepare the pasta, place the flour in a mixing bowl and make a well in the centre. Add the eggs, salt and oil and mix well. Mix in the sieved spinach and knead the dough. Set aside to rest for about 30 minutes.

Roll out the dough fairly thickly and cut into 8-cm/3-inch squares.

Bring a wide, shallow pan of lightly salted water to the boil. Lower the squares, 5 or 6 at a time, into the water and cook for 7-8 minutes, or until *al dente*. Remove the squares with a slotted spatula and spread out to cool on a warm, slightly damp cloth.

Grease an ovenproof dish with 2 tsp of the butter. Preheat the oven to 220° C/ 425° F, gas mark 7.

Arrange a layer of pasta squares on the bottom and pour over half the Bolognese sauce. Heat half the remaining butter and lightly sauté the chopped chicken. Scatter half the chicken over the Bolognese sauce. Sprinkle over some of the Parmesan cheese and shave a little truffle on to the surface, if using.

Arrange another layer of the pasta squares on top. Continue making layers in this way, finishing with a layer of pasta. Sprinkle over the remaining Parmesan cheese. Melt the remaining butter and drizzle it over.

Bake in the oven for 10-15 minutes, until the cheese has turned golden.

Serve immediately with extra grated Parmesan cheese handed separately.

Top: Fettucine Piedmont Style
Bottom: Lasagna alla Marchese

RICE

Rice is an important food because it is healthy, easily digestible, has high calorific value and yet is cheap. In Italy, it is used almost exclusively in the north.

The Italians cook rice in a very specific and characteristic way, not necessarily similar to that of other cuisines. You will need a pan large enough to hold a quantity of water four to five times the weight of the rice. Thus, for 500 g/1 lb 2 oz rice, you will need 1-3 litres/3½-4 pints water. The quality of the rice will determine the length of cooking time, but it will be about 15-20 minutes. The better the rice, the longer it will take to cook.

RICE WITH PEAS VENETIAN STYLE

Serves 6

170 ml/6 fl oz oil
30 g/1 oz butter
120 g/4 oz Parma ham or streaky bacon, diced
1 small onion, finely chopped
2-3 sprigs parsley, chopped
1.5 kg/3¼ lb peas (unshelled weight), shelled
salt
freshly ground black pepper
600 ml-1.1 litres/1-2 pints light stock
500 g/1 lb 2 oz rice
2 tbsp grated Parmesan cheese

Heat the oil and half the butter in a large saucepan. Add the diced ham or bacon,

onion and parsley. Fry gently for a few minutes and then add the peas. Season with salt and pepper and add a little stock. Bring to the boil, then add the rice.

Add enough stock to cover the rice, bring back to the boil and simmer until the rice is cooked, about 15-20 minutes. Season with pepper, add the remaining butter, and sprinkle over the Parmesan cheese before serving.

RISOTTO ALLA MILANESE

Serves 6

90 g/3 oz butter
1 tbsp beef marrow
1 medium Spanish onion, thinly sliced
500 g/1 lb 2 oz rice, washed and drained
600 ml-1.1 litres/1-2 pints chicken stock
salt
freshly ground black pepper
2 pinches saffron (optional)
170 g/6 oz ham, diced
60 g/2 oz grated Parmesan cheese

Garnish:
1 tbsp chopped parsley
1 tomato, cut into thin strips

Heat the butter in a large saucepan, add the marrow and onion and cook over low heat to soften the onion. Add the rice and stir thoroughly to ensure the rice is well coated and does not stick.

Bring the stock to the boil and begin

adding it gradually to the rice. Season with salt and pepper. After 3-4 minutes, add the saffron, if using, and stir it in well. By the time the last of the stock has been added and boiled to the point of evaporation, the rice will have cooked through. Add the remaining butter, stir in the ham and sprinkle over the Parmesan cheese. Serve garnished with finely chopped parsley and slivers of tomato, if liked.

Note: Risotto, which means 'little rice', is prepared in numerous ways, although the rice is always sautéed, together with chopped onion, in oil before it is cooked in stock. Risotto alla Milanese and risottos prepared with meat or seafood may be served as a main course, whereas those garnished simply with cheese or saffron are usually served as an accompaniment. Some risottos may be set in moulds. The recipe illustrated here has been set in a mould lined with thinly sliced tomato (see below).

GENOESE RICE

Serves 6

4 tbsp oil
1 small onion, diced
100 g/3½ oz mushrooms, chopped
250 g/9 oz tomatoes, skinned, seeded and diced
500 g/1 lb 2 oz rice, washed and drained
salt
freshly ground black pepper
60 g/2 oz cheese, grated

Heat the oil in a large, heavy-based saucepan or shallow, flameproof casserole. Sauté the onion for 5-7 minutes, until just coloured. Add the mushrooms and cook for 2-3 minutes. Add the tomatoes and cook for a further 5 minutes.

Cook the rice in lightly salted boiling water for 5 minutes. Remove from the heat, strain and add to the pan of vegetables. Cover the rice with boiling water, bring back to the boil and, after 5 minutes, season with salt and pepper and add the grated cheese.

Cook for a further 5 minutes, stirring constantly to prevent the rice from sticking to the pan.

Risotto alla Milanese

GNOCCHI

Gnocchi are perhaps the most ancient and primitive form of pasta. It seems likely that they were introduced to Italy by the Arabs in the Middle Ages.

Initially, they were prepared simply with water and flour; the addition of potato came much later. Today, after their fame and usage have spread throughout Italy, they are prepared with flour, potato, polenta or semolina and in all sorts of shapes and sizes.

Gnocchi means 'lumps' and they may well be related to other European dumplings, such as *knödel*, *noques*, *knepfle* and *quenelles*.

Gnocchi represent home cooking at its most traditional – and they are quick and easy to prepare.

POTATO GNOCCHI GENOVESE

Serves 6

2 kg/4¹/₂ lb potatoes, peeled
salt
500 g/1 lb 2 oz flour

Pesto:
9 garlic cloves
2-3 tbsp chopped basil
2 tbsp grated Pecorino cheese
3 tbsp grated Parmesan cheese
2 tbsp olive oil

Cook the potatoes in lightly salted boiling water for 20-25 minutes. Drain and mash thoroughly. Set aside to cool. When cool, turn out the mashed potatoes on to a work surface and knead thoroughly, adding the flour a little at a time, to obtain a soft dough.

With lightly floured hands, break off pieces of dough, form them into sausage shapes and then cut into 2.5-cm/1-inch thick slices. Hold one chunk in your hand, press the tines of a fork against the dough, and allow the gnocchi to drop on to a lightly floured cloth. It will form a hollow sausage shape. Repeat with the remaining slices.

To make the pesto, pound the garlic with the basil and a pinch of salt with a pestle in a mortar. Add the Pecorino and Parmesan cheeses and the oil, little by little, as you pound. Finally, blend the mixture into a thoroughly combined,

smooth paste with a wooden spoon.

Bring a pan of lightly salted water to the boil and add a few of the gnocchi. Allow them to float to the surface, cook for a further 3-4 minutes, then remove with a slotted spoon. Place the cooked gnocchi in individual soup plates. Cook the remaining gnocchi in the same way.

Dilute the pesto with a little of the cooking water and pour over the gnocchi. Serve immediately.

FLOUR GNOCCHI

Serves 6

100 g/3¹/₂ oz butter
1 small onion, chopped
250 g/9 oz bread, crusts removed, chopped
1 litre/1³/₄ pint milk, warmed
200 g/7 oz flour
salt
2-3 pinches saffron
5 egg yolks
170 g/6 oz fatty Parma ham or streaky bacon, rinds removed
1.1-1.7 litres/2-3 pints chicken stock

Top: Flour Gnocchi
Bottom: Potato Gnocchi Genovese

Melt the butter in a saucepan, add the chopped onion and bread and cook until the onion is lightly coloured. Remove from the heat, add the warmed milk and set aside until it has been completely absorbed, about 10 minutes.

Add the flour, salt, saffron and egg yolks, and mix well to make a dough. Allow to cool, then roll out on a board or a marble slab. The dough should be thick enough to make finger-thick gnocchi of whatever length you wish. See the previous recipe, Potato Gnocchi Genovese, for the method of preparing gnocchi, using a fork.

Bring the stock to the boil in a large pan and add the gnocchi. Simmer for at least 20 minutes, then serve in the broth.

Alternatively, make a meat sauce with an onion base. Pour this over the gnocchi, sprinkle with grated cheese and finish in a hot oven at 220° C/425° F, gas mark 7 for 10-15 minutes.

PIZZA

Pizza is a dish common to a number of regions in Italy. It is a family dish based on bread dough, which is then finished by adding any of a vast range of toppings.

This dish, particularly Pizza Napolitana, has found fame all over the world and the pizzeria is to be found virtually everywhere in the western world.

The secret of a successful pizza is in the preparation of the dough; it is always preferable, therefore, to make it fresh at home. The method is really very straightforward. The proportion of yeast to flour is 30 g/1 oz fresh yeast or 15 g/½ oz dried yeast to 500 g/1 lb 2 oz flour. Mix the yeast with a little tepid water to activate it. Make a ring of flour on a board and pour the yeast into the centre. Mix thoroughly and begin to knead, gradually adding more warm water, up to about 225 ml/8 fl oz.

Continue to knead vigorously, so that the dough becomes smooth, elastic and quite soft. Shape the dough into a ball and place it in a lightly floured bowl. Cover and set aside in a warm place to rise. The dough should double in size in an hour. For best results, turn out the dough, knock it back by kneading with your fists, return to the bowl and leave in a warm place for a further 20-30 minutes to double in size again.

PIZZA NAPOLITANA WITH SALAMI

Serves 6

90 g/3 oz butter
500 g/1 lb 2 oz pizza dough (see above)
2 eggs
2-3 tbsp warm water
salt
freshly ground black pepper
150 g/5 oz Mozzarella cheese, diced
100 g/3½ oz salami, diced
2 hard-boiled eggs, shelled and chopped

Preheat the oven to 230° C/450° F, gas mark 8. Grease a 23-cm/9-inch baking tin with 30 g/1 oz of the butter.

Place the dough in a mixing bowl and beat in the remaining butter, the eggs and the warm water. Season with salt and pepper. Knead the mixture vigorously, dropping it into the bowl occasionally, pounding it and finally stretching it out.

Left: Tuna and Tomato Pizza
Right: Pizza Napolitana with Salami

Divide the dough into two pieces and stretch out one piece into the prepared tin. Sprinkle over the diced mozzarella, salami and chopped hard-boiled eggs.

Cover this with the remainder of the dough, stretched to fit. Seal the edges firmly, so that the filling cannot seep out. Cover with a tea-towel and set aside to stand for about 20 minutes, until the dough has risen to the rim of the baking tin.

Bake in the oven for about 30 minutes. If

necessary, reduce the temperature to 200° C/400° F, gas mark 6 towards the end of the cooking time.

Remove from the oven and serve.

TUNA AND TOMATO PIZZA

Serves 6

60 g/2 oz lard, softened
700 g/1½ lb pizza dough (see page 28)
salt
freshly ground black pepper
1 kg/2¼ lb tomatoes, skinned, seeded and chopped
2-3 tbsp oil

200 g/7 oz canned tuna in oil, drained and flaked
225 g/8 oz fresh anchovies or sardines, cleaned, spines removed and chopped or 60 g/2 oz canned anchovy fillets, rinsed and chopped
100 g/3½ oz black olives, stoned and halved
1 tbsp capers

Preheat the oven 230° C/450° F, gas mark 8. Grease two 30-cm/12-inch baking tins with 1 tbsp of the lard.

Place the dough in a mixing bowl and beat in the remaining lard. Season with salt and pepper and knead vigorously. When thoroughly mixed together, divide the

dough into two parts and use to line the prepared baking tins.

Heat the oil and fry the tomatoes over high heat. When they are cooked, but not disintegrating, remove with a slotted spoon and set aside to cool. Mix together the tomatoes, flaked tuna, anchovy fillets, olives and capers and spread over the dough, dividing it equally between the two pizzas.

Bake for 30 minutes, until the crusts turn golden. Serve immediately.

This pizza is equally good eaten cold.

Note: The dough may also be used to make a 'pizza pie' like the Pizza Napolitana (opposite).

FRITTATE

Deep-frying is a method of preparing food that is found all over the Mediterranean. Although oil is generally used, pork fat and even butter are also common. It is important to note that a variety of temperatures is used to obtain different results with different types of ingredients. For example, moderate heat is best for frying anything with a high water content, such as all vegetables and fruit. Greater heat is required for anything where the initial contact with the oil or fat seals the outside and protects the inner flesh from overcooking. Obviously, this is a rapid process. Still more rapid is frying at a very high temperature for a very short time; this method is suitable for delicate ingredients, such as very small fish.

Savoury frittate may be served as either a first or, with vegetables or salad, as a second course.

CROQUETTES ROMANA

Serves 6

1 large onion, sliced
170 g/6 oz butter
300 g/10 oz cooked chicken, boned,
  skinned and diced
250 g/9 oz cooked tongue, diced
salt
150 g/5 oz flour, sifted
500 ml/18 fl oz milk
60 g/2 oz Parmesan cheese, grated
pinch grated nutmeg
2 eggs, lightly beaten
60 g/2 oz breadcrumbs

oil for deep-frying

Garnish:
3 lemons, cut into wedges

Melt 60 g/2 oz of the butter and sauté the onion. Gradually add the meat. Season, stir thoroughly and continue frying very gently over low heat.

Meanwhile, melt the remaining butter in a saucepan. Add the flour and cook, stirring constantly, for 2 minutes, until lightly coloured. Remove the pan from the heat and gradually stir in the milk. Return the pan to the heat and bring to the boil, stirring constantly. Add the Parmesan cheese and season with salt and nutmeg. Simmer gently for 1 minute,

remove from the heat and set aside to cool completely.

Heat the oil in a deep-fryer to 190° C/ 375° F, or until a cube of stale bread turns golden in 30 seconds.

When both the meat mixture and the sauce have cooled, mix them together. Using two teaspoons or with your hands, shape the mixture into small, oval balls. Coat the croquettes first in the beaten eggs and then in breadcrumbs. Fry until golden.

Remove and drain the croquettes. Transfer to a warm serving dish and garnish with the lemon wedges. Serve immediately.

CROQUETTES BOLOGNESE

Serves 6

75 g/2¹/2 oz butter
500 g/1 lb 2 oz lean roast veal, diced
120 g/4 oz Parma ham or streaky bacon,
  rinds removed and diced
150 ml/5 fl oz thick Béchamel sauce (see
  Tomato Soufflé, page 8)
salt
freshly ground black pepper
2 eggs, lightly beaten
2 egg yolks, beaten
45 g/1¹/2 oz Parmesan cheese, grated
75 g/2¹/2 oz black truffles, finely chopped
  (optional)
pinch nutmeg
3 tbsp flour
60 g/2 oz breadcrumbs

oil for deep-frying

Garnish:
3 lemons, cut into wedges

Melt the butter over moderate heat and stir in the meat. Stir in the Béchamel sauce and season with salt and pepper. Add half the beaten eggs and both the beaten yolks, stir thoroughly and allow the mixture to warm through. Remove the pan from the heat and pour the mixture into a large mixing bowl. Add the Parmesan cheese and most of the truffles, if using. (Reserve some pieces of truffle for garnishing, if liked.) Season with the nutmeg and set aside to cool completely.

Heat the oil in a deep-fryer to 190° C/375° F, or until a cube of stale bread turns golden in 30 seconds.

With two teaspoons or using your hands, shape the mixture into small balls. Dredge the croquettes with the flour, then coat first with the remaining beaten egg and then the breadcrumbs. Fry until golden and crisp.

Remove the croquettes from the oil and drain. Pile them on to a warm serving dish and garnish with the lemon wedges. Serve immediately.

FRITTATA WITH MOZZARELLA

Serves 6

60 g/2 oz butter
3-4 tbsp bread cubes
6 eggs
salt
freshly ground black pepper
100 g/3¹/2 oz Mozzarella cheese, diced

Melt the butter in a frying-pan and fry the bread cubes until they turn golden.

Beat the eggs, season with salt and pepper and add the diced Mozzarella cheese. As soon as the bread begins to colour, add the egg mixture to the pan. Continue to cook, stirring constantly, but do not allow the frittata to harden. Serve immediately.

Top: Croquettes Bolognese
Bottom: Frittata with Mozzarella

EGGS

Eggs are indispensible and used in many different dishes and for a wide range of culinary purposes. They are nutritious, fairly low in calories and easily digested. Eggs are tasty served on their own and can be prepared quickly as a snack – a boon to busy families.

In fact, there are fewer basic methods of preparing eggs than might, at first, be thought. Virtually all egg recipes are variations on about nine or ten basic techniques.

If in doubt about the freshness of an egg, plunge it into cold salted water. Fresh eggs – up to three days old – will sink to the bottom, older eggs will 'hang' in the water halfway up the container and bad eggs will float on the top.

PURGATORY EGGS

Serves 6

75 ml/2¹/₂ fl oz oil
1 small onion, chopped
1 kg/2¹/₄ lb tomatoes, skinned, seeded and chopped
1 tbsp tomato purée
salt
freshly ground black pepper
1 tbsp chopped parsley
12 eggs
2 tbsp grated Parmesan cheese

Heat the oil in a flameproof casserole or large gratin dish and sauté the onion for 5-7 minutes. When it starts to colour, add the tomatoes and tomato purée, season with salt and pepper and add a little water if necessary. Reduce the heat to low and simmer for about 30 minutes until the mixture has reduced to a thick sauce.

Stir in the chopped parsley. Break the eggs over the sauce and cook over a high heat until the whites are set but the yolks are still runny. Sprinkle over the Parmesan cheese and serve immediately.

RICE OMELETTE

Serves 6

100 g/3¹/₂ oz rice, rinsed
salt
30 g/1 oz butter
3 tbsp grated Parmesan cheese

60 g/2 oz salami, chopped
60 g/2 oz Gruyère cheese, diced
2 tbsp oil
6 eggs

Cook the rice in lightly salted boiling water for 15 minutes. Drain and add the butter, Parmesan cheese, chopped salami and diced Gruyère cheese.

Heat the oil in a 25-cm/10-inch frying-pan. Meanwhile, beat the eggs together and season with salt. When the oil is very hot and almost smoking, pour in the beaten egg.

Tilt the pan to distribute the egg evenly and stir once or twice. Cook the omelette, shaking the pan from time to time to make sure it does not stick. When it is almost cooked through but still runny on the surface, add the rice mixture and fold over the omelette.

Transfer the omelette to a warm serving dish by sliding it out of the pan.
Serve immediately.

EGGS BORGHESE

Serves 6

90 g/3 oz butter
1 medium onion, very finely sliced
1.5 kg/3¹/₄ lb tomatoes, skinned, seeded and chopped
salt
freshly ground black pepper
12 eggs
300 g/10 oz Gruyère cheese, diced
12 slices toast

Melt 1 tbsp of the butter in non-stick pan. Add the onion, cover and sauté until it colours. Add the tomatoes and season with salt and pepper. Increase the heat slightly and cook for 20 minutes, or until the mixture has reduced to a thick sauce.

Beat the eggs together and add the diced Gruyère cheese. Add the egg mixture to the sauce and cook until the cheese has melted.

Spread the remaining butter on the toast and place two slices on each of 6 individual plates. Divide the egg mixture between them and serve immediately.

EGGS FLORENTINE

Serves 6

500 g/1 lb 2 oz spinach
120 g/4 oz butter
120 ml/4 fl oz milk
salt
freshly ground black pepper
6 anchovy fillets, soaked in milk and drained
12 eggs
2-3 tbsp grated Parmesan cheese

Pastry:
100 g/3¹/₂ oz flour
90 g/3 oz butter
3 tbsp water

First make the pastry. Sift the flour into a mixing bowl. Dice 60 g/2 oz of the butter and rub it into the flour until the mixture resembles fine breadcrumbs. Add enough water to bind to a smooth dough. Cover and set aside in the refrigerator for 30 minutes to rest.

Preheat the oven 190°C/375°F, gas mark 5. Grease a 12-hole tartlet mould with the remaining butter.

Roll out the dough evenly and thinly. Cut out 12 rounds and use to line the tartlet mould. Fill with baking beans or crumpled foil and bake 'blind' for 10-12 minutes.

Meanwhile, wash the spinach and cut away any coarse stalks. Cook the spinach in just the water clinging to the leaves for 7-8 minutes. Drain and squeeze out all excess water, using your hands if necessary. Chop finely.

Melt 30 g/1 oz butter and gently heat the spinach. Add the milk and season with salt and pepper.

Remove the tartlets from the oven and discard the beans or foil. Put a large spoonful of spinach in each tartlet case. Arrange the tartlets on a flameproof dish.

Melt the remaining butter and make a paste by mashing the anchovies into it. Spread the paste over the spinach.

Poach the eggs in an egg poacher and place each egg on a bed of spinach. Sprinkle over the Parmesan cheese and put under a hot grill or into a hot oven for a 3-4 minutes. Serve immediately.

Top: Purgatory Eggs
Bottom: Rice Omelette

MIRELLA HARD-BOILED EGGS

Serves 6

9 hard-boiled eggs, shelled and halved
150 g/5 oz canned tuna, drained
3 anchovy fillets, chopped
1 tbsp chopped parsley
1 tbsp capers
75 ml/2¹/₂ fl oz mayonnaise
30 g/1 oz butter
2 small ripe tomatoes, sliced
2 small beetroot, finely chopped
salt
freshly ground black pepper
3 tbsp oil
1 tsp white wine vinegar

Scoop out the yolks of the eggs, taking
care not to damage the whites.
   Blend together the tuna, anchovies,
parsley, 9 capers, egg yolks, mayonnaise
and butter into a smooth paste. Fill the egg
whites with the mixture and decorate each
one with 2–3 capers.
   Place the eggs on a serving dish and
garnish with slices of tomato and shredded
beetroot. Season with salt, pepper, oil and
a little vinegar and serve.

**Left: Eggs Florentine
Above: Mirella Hard-Boiled Eggs**

FISH

Italian cooking makes use of the abundant variety of fish to be found in the Mediterranean and Adriatic Seas surrounding the peninsula and islands and in its rivers and lakes. There are so many recipes from all the regions that, for obvious reasons of limited space, we can only include a few of the most popular.

Top: Conger Eel Genovese
Bottom: Elvers Roman Style

ELVERS ROMAN STYLE

Serves 6

1 kg/2¼ lb elvers or whitebait, heads removed
3 tbsp oil
4 shallots or small onions, finely chopped
½ garlic clove, finely chopped
salt
freshly ground black pepper
100 ml/3½ fl oz white wine
1 tbsp tomato purée
500 g/1 lb 2 oz shelled peas

Wash and cut the elvers or whitebait into 5-cm/2-inch pieces, if necessary.

Heat the oil and fry the shallots and garlic over low heat for 5-7 minutes, until lightly coloured. Add the elvers or whitebait, season with salt and pepper and cook over low heat for 3-5 minutes.

Add the wine, stir in the tomato purée and add the peas. Stir thoroughly, cover and cook for 10-15 minutes.

CONGER EEL GENOVESE

Serves 6

1 kg/2¼ lb conger eel
200 ml/7 fl oz oil
1 small onion, diced
6 canned anchovy fillets, rinsed
500 g/1 lb 2 oz mushrooms, sliced
salt
freshly ground black pepper
100 ml/3½ fl oz dry white wine
2 garlic cloves
500 g/1 lb 2 oz shelled peas
1 tbsp tomato purée

Clean the eel, cut it into 4-cm/1½-inch slices and rinse thoroughly under cold running water. Pat dry and set aside.

Heat the oil in a flameproof casserole and gently fry the onion and anchovies for 5-7 minutes. Add the eel and the mushrooms, season with salt and pepper and cook for 3-4 minutes. Add the wine, the garlic cloves and the peas. Cover and cook gently until the wine has reduced almost completely.

Add the tomato purée and a little water. Cover, return to low heat and cook for a further 5 minutes or until tender.

SARDINIAN TUNA

Serves 6

1 kg/2¼ lb fresh tuna, in one large slice
100 ml/3½ fl oz wine vinegar
6 anchovy fillets
100 ml/3½ fl oz oil
60 g/2 oz butter
1 medium onion, chopped
1 carrot, chopped

1 stalk celery, chopped
4 dried mushrooms, soaked in warm water,
    drained and chopped
1 bay leaf
2 tbsp tomato purée
1 beef stock cube
100 ml/3½ fl oz dry white wine
1 egg yolk
juice of 1 lemon

Skin the tuna and place it in a deep dish. Add the vinegar and enough water to cover. Set aside for 2 hours.

Remove the tuna from the marinade, drain and pat dry. 'Lard' the tuna with the anchovy fillets.

Heat the oil with the butter in a flameproof casserole. Add the onion, carrot, celery, mushrooms and bay leaf and cook over high heat for 3-5 minutes. Add the tuna fillet and cook for 2-3 minutes on each side until browned on both sides. Add the tomato purée and simmer for 3 minutes. Crumble the cube into a little water and add to the casserole with the wine. Cover and cook for 20 minutes.

Transfer the tuna to a warm serving dish. Return the casserole to the heat and boil the sauce until it has reduced a little. Strain the sauce into a saucepan and reserve the mushrooms. Set the saucepan over low heat and stir in the egg yolk. Continue heating gently, stirring constantly, until the sauce has thickened slightly. Stir in the lemon juice and reserved mushrooms, pour over the tuna and serve immediately.

CALABRIAN RED MULLET

Serves 6

12 x 100 g/3½ oz red mullet, cleaned
100 ml/3½ fl oz oil
salt
juice of 1 lemon
1 tbsp chopped oregano

Preheat the oven to 200° C/400° F gas mark 6.

Scale the mullet. Wash and pat dry. Brush an ovenproof dish with oil and arrange the mullet in it. Season with salt,

Top: Sardinian Tuna
Bottom: Calabrian Red Mullet

lemon juice and oregano. Pour the rest of the oil over the fish, making sure they are all well coated. Bake in the oven for 10-15 minutes, or until the fish are cooked through. Serve at once.

SOLE BOLOGNESE

Serves 6

6 x 150-170 g/5-6 oz sole, cleaned
4 tbsp flour

2 eggs, beaten
200 ml/7 fl oz plus 1 tbsp oil
30 g/1 oz butter
250 g/9 oz canned artichoke hearts, drained
    and sliced
120 g/4 oz mushrooms, diced
2 medium potatoes, boiled, drained and sliced
salt
juice of 2 lemons

Remove the dark skin from the sole. Wash and pat dry. Dredge the sole with the flour and coat with the beaten eggs.

Heat 200 ml/7 fl oz of the oil in a frying-pan and fry the sole over high heat until golden and crispy on both sides. Set aside and keep warm.

Melt the butter with the remaining oil in another large deep-frying pan. Add the artichoke hearts, diced mushrooms and sliced potatoes. Mix well, and season with salt and lemon juice.

Place the golden, crispy sole in the pan and allow to cook for several minutes to absorb all the flavours. Transfer the sole and the sauce to a warm serving dish and serve immediately.

BABY SQUID NAPOLITANA

Serves 6

1 kg/2¹/₄ lb baby squid
2-3 tbsp oil
1 garlic clove, crushed
500 g/1 lb 2 oz tomatoes, skinned, seeded and
  chopped
salt
freshly ground black pepper
30 g/1 oz pine nuts
60 g/2 oz black olives, stoned
30 g/1 oz raisins

Garnish:
3 slices white bread
2 tbsp butter
1 tbsp chopped parsley

If you are using fresh squid, they must be cleaned. Remove the head, tentacles, guts, ink sac and transparent quill. Remove all traces of membrane. Alternatively, you can use ready-prepared fresh or frozen squid.

Heat the oil in a large frying-pan. Add the garlic and cook for 3-5 minutes, until lightly coloured. Stir in the tomatoes, season with salt and pepper and cook for 5 minutes.

Add the squid, pine nuts, olives and raisins. Cook over gentle heat for no longer than 10-15 minutes – squid becomes unpleasantly rubbery if it is overcooked.

Meanwhile, cut the bread into crescent shapes with a biscuit cutter and toast lightly or fry in butter to make croûtons.

Transfer the squid mixture to a warm serving dish, sprinkle over the parsley and serve garnished with the toast or crescent croûtons.

Left: Baby Squid Napolitana
Right: Sole Bolognese

MEAT

Meat and meat products are valuable sources of nutrition, particularly for children and adolescents, who require a relatively high intake of protein and vitamins during the critical period of growth. Meat contains about 20 per cent protein, including many essential amino acids. However, it tends to be rich in saturated fats – even lean meats containing as much as 10 per cent fat – so moderation is advisable. Meat contains many minerals, particularly iron, and vitamins of the B complex. Unlike many other foods, these are mainly retained during cooking.

Meat is usually classified into three categories. Red meat includes beef and lamb, white meat includes poultry, rabbit, pork and veal, and dark meat or game includes venison, boar and all the game birds, such as pheasant grouse, partridge, pigeon and quail.

The main distinction between these categories is the meat's digestibility. White meat is usually considered most suitable for people who are ill, frail or convalescing. In general, the digestibility of meat is affected by the species of the animal, its age, sex and diet, the particular cut which is chosen, its freshness and, of course, the way it is cooked.

Meat does not have such a major role in the traditional Italian daily diet as it does in Northern Europe and the United States. For the peasants of the past, the slaughtering of a pig – often their only source of meat – was a special and festive occasion. More conventional celebrations, such as Christmas and Easter, was also characterized by an abundance of meat dishes. As Italy is mainly a Catholic country, Lent is taken seriously and many families do not eat meat or meat products throughout the entire 40 days. Consequently, the celebrations on Easter Sunday include especially rich and delicious meals, often featuring lamb.

SICILIAN FILLET OF BEEF

Serves 6

3-4 tbsp oil
1 garlic clove, chopped
1 celery stalk, chopped
6 x 150-170 g/5-6 oz fillet steaks
2 tomatoes, skinned, seeded and chopped
100 g/3¹/₂ oz green olives, stoned

3 tbsp capers
3 small gherkins, chopped and seeded
salt
freshly ground black pepper
1 tsp chopped oregano
1 tbsp red wine vinegar

Heat the oil in frying-pan. Fry the chopped garlic for about 3-5 minutes and then remove it from the pan as soon as it begins to colour.

Sauté the chopped celery for 5 minutes, or until it softens. Remove from the pan and reserve.

Increase the heat and fry the steaks on both sides until they are half done. Add the tomatoes, olives, capers, chopped gherkins and reserved celery. Season with salt and pepper and add the oregano. Stir in the wine vinegar and continue to fry until the meat is cooked to your taste. Test the edge of the steak with a sharp knife to check whether it is rare, medium or well done.

Note: For a classic Sicilian flavour, the olives should be preserved in brine and fennel. These may be available from some Italian delicatessen stores.

SALTIMBOCCA

Serves 6

6 x 100 g/3¹/₂ oz veal escalopes
60 g/2 oz Parma ham
1 sage sprig
salt
freshly ground black pepper
2-3 tbsp white wine
90 g/3 oz butter

Try to buy veal which has already been tenderized by being beaten very thin. If you cannot, then place the escalopes on a wooden board, cover with greaseproof paper and beat with a rolling pin or the smooth side of a steak mallet until they are 5 mm/¹/₄ inch thick.

Using a cocktail stick, secure a piece of the ham and 1-2 sage leaves to each escalope, as if pinning together two pieces of fabric. Season the escalopes with salt and pepper to taste, but be careful not to add too much salt as the ham will also season the veal.

Melt 60 g/2 oz of the butter in a frying-pan. Fry the escalopes over high heat for 2 minutes on each side or just long enough to brown the meat slightly.

Remove the escalopes from the frying-pan and transfer to a warm serving dish. Add the wine to the pan and increase the heat. Add the remaining butter and stir vigorously. Pour the deglazed sauce over the meat and serve immediately.

Note: Saltimbocca means 'jump into the mouth' – because it is so delicious. It originated in Brescia but is now thought of as a Roman speciality.

ROMAN MEATBALLS

Makes 18 meatballs

600 g/1¹/₄ lb lean minced beef or leftover boiled or roast beef, minced
60 g/2 oz pork fat, finely diced
60 g /2 oz streaky bacon, rinds removed and finely diced
2 tbsp chopped parsley
salt
freshly ground black pepper
¹/₂ tsp grated nutmeg
120 g/4 oz white bread, crusts removed
1 egg, lightly beaten
2 tbsp raisins
2 tbsp pine nuts
2 tbsp grated Parmesan cheese
2-3 tbsp breadcrumbs
200 ml/7 fl oz oil

In a mixing bowl, combine the minced beef, diced pork fat, bacon and parsley. Season with salt, pepper and add the grated nutmeg.

Put the bread in a bowl and pour over just enough water to cover. Set aside to soak for about 10 minutes and then squeeze out as much moisture as possible. Add to the bowl of meat and mix all the ingredients thoroughly by kneading together by hand. Add the egg, raisins, pine nuts and grated Parmesan cheese. Mix well and shape into balls the size of small apples by rolling the mixture between the palms of your hands. Flatten the tops slightly.

Roll the meatballs in the breadcrumbs to

Top: Saltimbocca
Bottom: Sicilian Fillet of Beef

coat them. Heat the oil in a frying-pan and fry the meatballs for 8-10 minutes, or until cooked through.

Serve immediately as they are or simmer for a few minutes in some light stock.

CALVES' KIDNEYS PARMA-STYLE

Serves 4

2 calves' kidneys
salt
freshly ground black pepper
150 g/5 oz butter
350 g/12 oz fresh asparagus tips, cooked or canned asparagus tips
60 g/2 oz Parmesan cheese, grated
100 ml/3¹/₂ fl oz Marsala or sweet white wine
100 ml/3¹/₂ fl oz strong meat stock (see page 14)

Preheat the oven to 200° C/400° F, gas mark 6.

Trim any fat from the kidneys, peel off the membrane and cut them in half lengthwise. Remove the spongy tissue from the inside, together with any blood vessels. Cut each half into three and season with salt and pepper.

Melt 60 g/2 oz of the butter. Lightly brush a baking dish with a little of the melted butter. Carefully arrange the asparagus tips in the dish, pour over the remaining melted butter and sprinkle over the Parmesan cheese. Place in the oven to gratinate for about 10 minutes.

Meanwhile, melt 60 g/2 oz of the remaining butter in a frying-pan. Add the kidneys and increase the heat. Cook for 7-8 minutes, until they are sealed but still pink inside. Remove from the pan, set aside and keep warm.

Deglaze the pan by adding the Marsala or wine. Increase the heat and stir. When the liquid has reduced by half, add the stock and continue to boil for a further few minutes, stirring constantly. Remove the pan from the heat, add the remaining butter and return the meat to the sauce.

Transfer the kidneys and sauce to a warm serving dish, garnish with the asparagus tips and serve immediately.

Left top: Calves' Kidneys Parma-Style
Left bottom: Calves' Liver Milanese

CALVES' LIVER MILANESE

Serves 6

100 ml/3¹/₂ fl oz oil
2 tbsp chopped parsley
salt
freshly ground black pepper
6 x 100 g/3¹/₂ oz slices calves' liver
2-3 tbsp flour
2 eggs, lightly beaten
100 g/3¹/₂ oz very fine breadcrumbs
100 g/3¹/₂ oz butter

Garnish:
1 lemon, cut into wedges
3 small tomatoes, halved

Tuscan Lamb with Peas (see page 44)

In a shallow dish mix together the oil and the parsley and season with salt and pepper. Add the slices of liver and set aside to marinate for 1 hour, turning them over halfway through the marination time.

Remove the liver from the marinade and drain. Coat the liver first with the flour, then with the beaten egg and finally with the breadcrumbs.

Melt the butter in a heavy frying-pan. Just before it turns brown, add the slices of liver and fry over a high heat until golden brown and crispy on the outside but still soft on the inside.

Garnish with the lemon and tomatoes, if using, and serve immediately.

TUSCAN LAMB WITH PEAS

Serves 4

1 x 1 kg/2¼ lb leg of lamb
4 garlic cloves, sliced
2-3 sprigs rosemary
2 tbsp oil
salt
freshly ground black pepper
500 g/1 lb 2 oz ripe tomatoes, skinned, seeded
   and finely chopped
2 tbsp water
500 g/1 lb 2 oz shelled peas

Make incisions in the meat with a sharp
knife to create 'pockets' and insert slivers
of garlic and 1-2 rosemary spikes in each.
Rub the meat all over with a little of the
oil and season with salt and pepper. Heat
the remaining oil in a flameproof casserole
and brown the meat all over.

   Add the tomatoes and the water to the
casserole. Bring to the boil, lower the
heat, cover and simmer for 45 minutes to
1 hour.

   Boil the peas in lightly salted water for
10 minutes, or until three-quarters
cooked. Drain and add to the meat 10
minutes before the end of the cooking
time. Alternatively, cook the peas for 20
minutes until tender. Drain and pile them
into a hollowed-out tomato and keep
warm.

   Transfer the lamb to a warm serving
dish, pour over the sauce and garnish with
the peas, if cooked separately. Serve
immediately.

TOURNEDOS LUIGI
VERONELLI

Serves 6

1 small onion, diced
1 small carrot, diced
170 g/6 oz butter
100 ml/3½ fl oz dry white wine
bouquet garni
75 ml/2½ fl oz tomato purée
salt
freshly ground black pepper
6 tbsp water
1 truffle, finely sliced
500 g/1 lb 2 oz mushrooms, sliced
60 ml/2 fl oz cognac
3-4 tbsp oil
6 beef fillet tournedos, 2.5 cm/1 inch thick
6 slices white bread
6 slices chicken liver pâté

Tournedos Luigi Veronelli

Melt 30 g/1 oz of the butter and fry the diced onion and carrot for 5-7 minutes over low heat until lightly coloured. Add the white wine and increase the heat slightly. When the liquid has reduced by half, add the bouquet garni and tomato purée and season with salt and pepper. Stir well, add the water and reduce the heat to very low. Simmer for about 1 hour. remove from the heat and strain.

Cut 6 small slices of truffle and reserve. Finely dice the remaining truffle.

Remove the wine sauce from the heat and strain. Add the diced truffle and 60 g/ 2 oz of the remaining butter. Keep warm in a *bain marie* or in a heatproof basin set over a pan of hot water.

Melt 30 g/1 oz of the remaining butter in a frying-pan and fry the mushrooms over very high heat for 2-3 minutes. When they are just cooked, reduce the heat and add the cognac. Ignite the cognac and shake the pan until the flames die down. Remove from the pan and set aside.

Melt 30 g/1 oz of the remaining butter with half the oil in the pan and fry the tournedos over high heat for 3-4 minutes on each side. Season with salt and pepper and set aside.

Cut the bread slices to the same shape and size, as the tournedos, but not to the same thickness. Heat the remaining butter with the remaining oil in the pan and fry the bread slices

Arrange the fried bread on a warm serving dish and top each slice with a tournedos. Garnish each tournedos with a slice of pâté and a slice of truffle. Pour over the sauce and garnish with the mushrooms. Serve immediately.

BOLOGNESE TRIPE

Serves 6

2 tbsp oil
120 g/4 oz belly of pork, finely chopped
1 small onion, finely chopped
1 garlic clove, finely chopped
1 tbsp chopped parsley
1 kg/2¼ lb cooked tripe, diced
salt
freshly ground black pepper
75 ml/2½ fl oz chicken stock
75 ml/2½ fl oz strong meat stock
2 egg yolks
120 g/4 oz Parmesan cheese, grated

Heat the oil in a flameproof casserole. Add the chopped belly of pork, onion, garlic and parsley and fry until lightly coloured.

Add the diced tripe to the casserole,

season with salt and pepper and cook for 2-3 minutes. Add the chicken stock and increase the heat. Bring to the boil, reduce the heat, cover and simmer for about 1 hour or until the pork is tender.

Remove the casserole from the heat. Warm the meat stock and blend with the egg yolks. Pour the stock and egg yolk mixture into the casserole, sprinkle over a little of the cheese and serve immediately. Serve the remaining grated Parmesan cheese separately.

The dish may be garnished with finely sliced tomato and onion, if liked.

Note: Do not keep the prepared dish warm over direct heat or the egg yolks may curdle the sauce.

OSSO BUCO

Serves 6

700 g/1½ lb veal shin, chopped into
  6 pieces
2-3 tbsp flour
120 g/4 oz butter
1 small onion, diced
1 celery stalk, diced
1 carrot, diced
1 tbsp chopped marjoram
2 garlic cloves, chopped
rind of 1 lemon, finely chopped
salt
freshly ground black pepper
100 ml/3½ fl oz dry white wine
2 ripe tomatoes, skinned, seeded and
  chopped
3-4 tbsp veal or chicken stock
rind of ¼ orange, finely chopped

Dredge the veal shin pieces with the flour. Melt 90 g/3 oz of the butter in a flameproof casserole and brown the meat on all sides.

Add the onion, celery, carrot, marjoram, half the garlic and three-quarters of the lemon peel to the casserole. Season with salt and pepper. Add the wine and increase the heat slightly. Cook until the wine is almost completely reduced.

Add the tomatoes and stock to the casserole. Reduce the heat to low, cover and simmer for at least 2 hours, adding a tablespoon of stock occasionally to dilute the sauce, if necessary. The meat should be very tender.

Ten minutes before serving, add the chopped orange peel the remaining lemon peel, the remaining garlic and the remaining butter. Stir well.

Serve the osso buco, covered in its sauce, with Risotto alla Milanese (see page 26).

Note: Osso buco means 'bone with a hole', a reference to the veal knuckle traditionally used in the preparation of this dish. This dish originated in Milan and is sometimes called Osso Buco Milanese. Authentic Osso Buco Milanese is always flavoured with lemon rind, but does not include tomatoes.

BRAISED BEEF BRESCIA-STYLE

Serves 6

90 g/3 oz pork fat
1 kg/2¼ lb braising steak, in one piece
salt
freshly ground black pepper
1 small onion, roughly chopped
1 garlic clove, crushed
90 g/3 oz butter
225 ml/8 fl oz red wine

Cut the pork fat into strips and use to lard the beef. Secure the strips in position with string, which will also help to keep the meat in shape. Season with salt and pepper to taste.

Place the larded beef in a flameproof casserole with the onion, garlic, butter and any pork fat that remains.

Brown the meat over moderate heat, turning it several times every 4-5 minutes. Keep the casserole tightly covered at all other times.

After 30 minutes, add the wine and cover again immediately. Cook over low heat, without adding any more liquid, for a further 45 minutes, until the meat is tender.

Serve accompanied by plain boiled pasta or rice and a green salad.

Bolognese Tripe

POULTRY

As in other countries throughout the Mediterranean, poultry plays a very important part in Italian cooking. The Italians make delicious use not only of chicken, but also of turkey, duck, goose and pigeon.They enjoy poussins (baby chickens) as much as large chickens and also eat turkey at Christmas, especially prizing the tender meat of the young turkey hen. Goose, which is rather heavy and fat, is less popular and, again, a young bird is preferred. Both domestic and wild duck are eaten; so, too, are young pigeon.

Hunting is a passion for many Italians. As well as red and grey partridge, quail and pheasant, all kinds of birds – some astonishingly small – find their way into the cooking pot.

ITALIAN STEWED DUCK

Serves 4

1 kg/2¼ lb duck, with giblets
200 ml/7 fl oz oil
75 ml/2½ fl oz wine vinegar
1 small onion, finely diced
2 garlic cloves, crushed
salt
freshly ground black pepper
100-225 ml/3½-8 fl oz red wine
225 ml/8 fl oz water
bouquet garni
1 tsp butter

Garnish:
grilled tomatoes

Cut the duck into pieces. Chop the giblets and place in a flameproof casserole. Add the duck pieces, oil, vinegar, onion and garlic. Season with salt and pepper to taste. Mix together the wine and water and pour enough into the casserole so that the duck is just covered. Add the bouquet garni.

Lightly grease a sheet of greaseproof paper with the butter and place on top. Cover the casserole with the lid and cook over very low heat for at least 1 hour.

Remove the casserole from the heat and transfer the duck pieces to a heated serving dish. Keep warm.

Return the casserole to low heat and reduce the remaining juices slightly. Strain the juices and pour over the duck. Garnish with grilled tomatoes and serve with barquettes filled with beans, if liked.

PIEDMONTESE QUAILS WITH RICE

Serves 6

12 quails
1-1.25 litres/1¾-2 pints chicken stock
350 g/12 oz rice
1 small onion, finely chopped
150 g/5 oz butter
salt
freshly ground black pepper
120 g/4 oz Parmesan cheese, grated
100 ml/3½ fl oz strong Italian meat stock
  (see page 14)
1 truffle, sliced

The fresher and plumper the quails the better. Ask your butcher to tie them so that they retain their shape.

In a saucepan, bring 1 litre/1¾ pints of the chicken stock to the boil, add the rice

and chopped onion. Cook for about 20 minutes, adding more boiling stock if necessary, until the rice is tender and the liquid has been completely absorbed. Stir in 60 g/2 oz butter and the Parmesan cheese and turn on to a warm serving dish.

Meanwhile, heat the remaining butter in a flameproof casserole, add the quails, increase the heat and brown them thoroughly on all sides. Add the meat stock to the casserole and heat through.

Arrange the quails on the rice and place the truffle slices on top. Serve before the quail lose too much heat. Garnish with crescents of puff pastry, if liked.

Left: Italian Stewed Duck
Right: Piedmontese Quails with Rice

VEGETABLES

Italian cuisine uses the abundant produce of the peninsula's kitchen gardens to the full. Vegetables are not simply used as a flavouring for other dishes, but often form the principal ingredient; nor are they simply served as an accompaniment to meat. Shopping for vegetables is an important part of the visit to any market, where the produce is touched and thoroughly inspected to ensure that it is at the peak of ripeness and in perfect condition. Needless to say, they are bought fresh each day. Italian cooks include all manner of plants in the category of 'vegetables' – roots, tubers, bulbs, leaves and even flowers and fruit.

PIZZAIOLA POTATOES

Serves 6

1 kg/2¼ lb floury potatoes (e.g. King Edward's)
salt
90 ml/3 fl oz oil
3-4 garlic cloves, finely chopped
500 g/1 lb 2 oz tomatoes, skinned, seeded and chopped
freshly ground black pepper
2 tsp chopped oregano

Boil the potatoes in lightly salted water for 20-25 minutes until just tender. Drain and peel.

Heat the oil and sauté the garlic for 3-5 minutes until lightly coloured. Add the tomatoes and season with salt and pepper and stir in the oregano. Cook over low heat for about 10 minutes. Add the potatoes, stir well and heat through.

Transfer to a warm serving dish and serve immediately.

ROMAN ARTICHOKES

Serves 6

12 fresh artichoke hearts
1 tsp wine vinegar
1 tbsp finely chopped mint
3-4 garlic cloves, finely chopped
60 g/2 oz breadcrumbs
salt
freshly ground black pepper
2-3 tbsp oil
225 ml/8 fl oz water

Place the artichoke hearts in a large shallow dish. Pour over enough cold water to cover and add the vinegar. Set aside for 30 minutes to soak.

Preheat the oven to 180° C/350° F, gas mark 4.

Make a paste by combining thoroughly the chopped mint, garlic, breadcrumbs, salt, pepper and 2 tbsp of the oil. Drain the artichoke hearts and, using a teaspoon, stuff them with this mixture.

Arrange the artichoke hearts in a flameproof casserole and pour over the remaining oil and the water. Season with a little more salt and pepper.

Cook in the oven for 1 hour, basting occasionally with the cooking juices.

Transfer the artichoke hearts to a serving dish and keep warm. Bring the remaining cooking liquid to the boil and cook until it has reduced by half.

Pour the sauce over the artichoke hearts and serve immediately.

Note: Artichokes are eaten all over Italy, but preparing them flavoured with mint is a typically Roman touch.

MILANESE SPINACH

Serves 6

1 kg/2¼ lb spinach, washed and stalks removed
70 g/2¼ oz butter
salt
freshly ground black pepper
60 g/2 oz Parmesan cheese, grated
12 fried eggs

Preheat the oven to 225° C/425° F, gas mark 7.

Cook the spinach in just the water clinging to its leaves for 8 minutes. Drain, refresh under cold water and squeeze out all the liquid.

Melt 60 g/2 oz of the butter in a gratin dish or other flameproof serving dish and add the spinach. Season with salt and pepper. Sprinkle over the cheese and dot with the remaining butter. Place in the oven for about 10 minutes to gratinate. Alternatively, place under a grill preheated to high.

Remove the dish from the oven and serve immediately accompanied with the freshly fried eggs.

SPINACH BAKE

Serves 6

3 dried mushrooms
1.5 kg/3¼ lb spinach, washed and stalks removed
300 ml/10 fl oz oil
2 small onions, finely sliced
1 tbsp chopped parsley
2 garlic cloves, chopped
3 eggs, lightly beaten
2 tbsp grated Parmesan cheese
salt
freshly ground black pepper
30 g/1 oz breadcrumbs

Put the mushrooms in a basin and pour over enough warm water to cover. Set aside for 20 minutes to soak.

Cut the spinach leaves into strips and cook in just the water clinging to the leaves for 8 minutes.

Drain the spinach, squeezing out the remaining moisture by hand.

Drain the mushrooms, rinse thoroughly and chop finely.

Heat 50 ml/2 fl oz of the oil in a large saucepan and fry the onion for 5-7 minutes until lightly coloured. Add the chopped parsley, garlic and mushrooms. Finally, add the spinach. Cook over low heat for 3-4 minutes. Remove the pan from the heat and set aside to cool.

Preheat the oven to 190° C/375° F, gas mark 5.

When the spinach mixture is cool, stir in the beaten eggs and half the Parmesan cheese. Add most of the remaining oil and season with salt and pepper.

Brush an ovenproof dish with the remaining oil and sprinkle over half the remaining cheese. Put the spinach mixture in the dish, spreading it flat with a spoon. Mix the remaining cheese with the breadcrumbs and sprinkle over the spinach mixture. Bake in the oven for about 10 minutes, until the top turns golden. Serve immediately.

Alternatively, remove the dish from the oven and set aside to cool completely before serving.

Top: Milanese Spinach
Bottom: Roman Artichokes

CAPONATA NAPOLITANA

Serves 6

1 large cauliflower
2 curly endives, chopped
150 g/5 oz pickled vegetables, chopped
100 g/3½ oz capers
100 g/3½ oz black olives, stoned
8 canned anchovy fillets, rinsed
9 tbsp olive oil
9 tbsp wine vinegar
2 tsp chopped oregano
salt
freshly ground black pepper
6 taralli (see page 56)
6 green olives, stoned

Cook the cauliflower in boiling, salted water for 15-20 minutes or until just tender. Drain and set aside to cool.

Divide the cauliflower into florets and arrange them on a serving dish, together with the chopped endives, pickles, capers and black olives. Add half the anchovies.

Mix together 7 tbsp of the oil, 3 tbsp of the vinegar and the oregano. Season with salt and pepper and pour over the salad.

Place the taralli in a dish. Mix together the remaining vinegar and 3 tbsp water and pour over the taralli. Set aside to soak, stirring occasionally.

When the taralli have softened, remove with a slotted spoon and place them on the salad. Pour over the remaining oil and garnish with the remaining anchovies and the stoned green olives.

Set the caponata aside for 1-2 hours before serving so that the flavours integrate thoroughly.

ITALIAN STUFFED CABBAGE

Serves 6

500 g/1 lb 2 oz green cabbage
45 g/1½ oz breadcrumbs
450ml/16 fl oz strong Italian meat stock (see page 14)
100 g/3½ oz butter
60 g/2 oz chicken livers
60 g/2 oz veal sweetbreads
100 g/3½ oz veal, sliced
1 tbsp grated Parmesan cheese
¼ tsp grated nutmeg
salt
freshly ground black pepper
1 egg yolk
450 ml/16 fl oz chicken stock

Trim the cabbage and cut out the heart. Bring a pan of lightly salted water to the boil and cook the whole cabbage for a few minutes. Remove, refresh with cold water and drain thoroughly.

Put the breadcrumbs in a bowl, pour over half the meat stock and set aside to soak.

Clean the chicken livers by removing as much membrane and greenish bile as possible without losing the shape. Make sure the sweetbreads are clean. Melt half the butter and fry the chicken livers, sweetbreads and veal slices for about 10 minutes until cooked. Remove from the heat and set aside to cool.

Finely chop the meat and place in a mixing bowl. Stir in the soaked breadcrumbs, Parmesan cheese and nutmeg. Season with salt, pepper and add the egg yolk, Mix thoroughly to form a paste.

Carefully separate the cabbage leaves without removing them, keeping the original shape as best you can. Put a spoonful of the meat mixture behind each leaf. Return the cabbage to its original shape and tie it in place with string to ensure the stuffing does not escape.

Heat the remaining meat stock with the remaining butter in a large saucepan. Add the cabbage and cook over a moderate heat for 10-15 minutes, adding a little of the chicken stock from time to time.

Remove the cabbage from the pan and discard the string. Cut into portions and place on a serving dish. Pour over the cooking juices and serve immediately.

Aromatic Kidney Bean Salad

AROMATIC KIDNEY BEAN SALAD

Serves 6

1 tbsp finely chopped basil
1 tbsp finely chopped parsley
100 ml/3½ fl oz wine vinegar
1 small onion
1 garlic clove, chopped
1 x 100 g/3½ oz can tuna in oil, drained
1 kg/2¼ lb kidney beans, soaked overnight in cold water and drained
12 canned anchovy fillets, rinsed
2 tbsp oil
salt
freshly ground black pepper

Mix together the basil and parsley in a salad bowl and pour over the vinegar.

Mince the onion and place it in a small cloth. Briefly hold under cold running water and squeeze out the liquid as forcefully as you can. Add the onion and the chopped garlic to the bowl. Flake the tuna with a fork and add to the bowl.

Put the kidneys beans in a pan of lightly salted boiling water. Bring back to the boil and boil vigorously for 10 minutes.★ Lower the heat and simmer for at least 40 minutes until the beans are cooked. Drain and set aside to cool. Alternatively, use canned cooked beans, rinsed and drained.

Add the beans and the anchovies to the bowl and mix well. Set aside for 4 hours for the flavours to mingle. Stir in the oil, season with salt and pepper and serve.

★Note: Make sure the kidney beans are boiled vigorously for 10 minutes as this destroys a toxin they contain.

SICILIAN BROCCOLI

Serves 6

700 g/1½ lb broccoli
60 g/2 oz black olives, stoned
12 canned anchovy fillets, rinsed and chopped
1 small onion, diced
60 g/2 oz Parmesan cheese, grated
225 ml/8 fl oz oil
salt
freshly ground black pepper
450 ml/16 fl oz red wine

Garnish:
12 olives, stoned
12 canned anchovy fillets
6 slices bread, crusts removed, fried in butter and cut into triangles

Top: Sicilian Broccoli
Bottom Sicilian Aubergines

Cut the broccoli into florets, discard the leaves and keep the central stalk. Wash and drain.

Combine the olives, chopped anchovies, diced onion and cheese.

Pour half the oil into a flameproof casserole and spread over a layer of the olive mixture. Arrange a layer of broccoli on top and season with salt and pepper. Continue making layers until all the ingredients have been used up. Pour over the remaining oil and add enough wine just to reach the surface.

Simmer over moderate heat for about 30 minutes or until the broccoli is cooked and the wine has evaporated.

Serve hot garnished with olives wrapped in anchovy fillets and accompanied by triangles of golden fried bread.

SICILIAN AUBERGINES

Serves 6

2-3 tbsp oil
6 medium aubergines, peeled and diced
salt
freshly ground black pepper
3 hard-boiled eggs, shelled and chopped
1 tbsp chopped basil
200 g/7 oz Mozzarella cheese, diced
100 g/3½ oz Parmesan cheese, grated
2 ripe tomatoes, skinned, seeded and chopped

Preheat the oven to 220° C/425° F, gas mark 7. Brush a large ovenproof casserole with 1 tsp of the oil.

Heat 2 tbsp of the remaining oil in a large frying-pan. Add the aubergines and

fry for about 8 minutes, turning once, until browned on both sides. Remove with a slotted spatula and drain on kitchen paper. Season lightly with salt and pepper.

Arrange half the aubergines in a layer on the bottom of the prepared casserole. Cover with a layer of chopped eggs, basil and Mozzarella cheese. Sprinkle over half the Parmesan cheese. Arrange the remaining aubergines on top, followed by the chopped tomatoes. Drizzle over the remaining oil and sprinkle over the remaining Parmesan cheese. Season with a little more salt and pepper.

Cover and bake in the oven for 15 minutes or until the cheese has browned. Serve immediately.

PRAWN, PEPPER AND RICE SALAD

Serves 6

350 g/12 oz rice
2 slices lemon
salt
350 g/12 oz uncooked prawns
3-4 tbsp olive oil
juice of 2 lemons
1 green pepper, halved and seeded
1 red pepper, halved and seeded
1 yellow pepper, halved and seeded
1 x 100 g/3$^{1}/_{2}$ oz can tuna in oil, drained
90 g/3 oz mushrooms, sliced
freshly ground black pepper

Bring a pan of lightly salted water to the boil. Add the lemon slices and the rice and cook for about 15 minutes until the rice is tender but not too soft.

Remove the pan from the heat, rinse the rice under cold water and drain.

Preheat the grill to high.

Cook the prawns in boiling water for about 3–5 minutes. Drain, peel and discard the shells. Season the prawns with salt, 1 tbsp of the oil and half the lemon juice.

Flatten the pepper halves with your hand. Place them under the grill and cook until the skin has blistered and blackened. Put them into a polythene bag, secure the top and set aside for about 15 minutes.

Meanwhile, heat 1 tbsp of the remaining oil and sauté the mushrooms for 4–6 minutes. Set aside to cool.

Peel the peppers and cut them into strips. Drizzle over 1 tbsp of the oil.

Arrange the rice on a serving dish. Flake the tuna with a fork and place it on top. Add the sliced mushrooms and peppers and top with the prawns. Season with oil, salt, pepper and lemon juice and serve.

Prawn, Pepper and Rice Salad

PARMA SPINACH MOULD

Serves 6

1 tbsp butter
500 g/1lb 2 oz spinach
200 ml/7 fl oz Béchamel sauce (see Tomato
  Soufflé, page 8)
4 eggs, lightly beaten
60 g/2 oz Parmesan cheese, grated
salt

Cream sauce :
200 ml/7 fl oz Béchamel sauce (see Tomato
  Soufflé, page 8)
90 ml/3 fl oz single cream
60 g/2 oz butter

Preheat the oven to 190° C/375° F, gas
mark 5. Grease an ovenproof dish or 6
individual moulds with the butter.

Blanch the spinach for 1 minute in
boiling water. Remove and refresh under
cold water, drain and purée it in a food
processor or food mill. Transfer the purée
to a pan and place over low heat.
Gradually add the Béchamel sauce, stirring
constantly. Remove the pan from the heat
and stir in the beaten eggs and Parmesan
cheese. Season with salt.

Pour the spinach mixture into the
prepared dish or moulds. Place the dish or
moulds in a roasting tin and pour around
enough hot water to come halfway up the
side of the dish or moulds. Bake in the
oven for 15 minutes.

Meanwhile, make the cream sauce. Mix
together the Béchamel sauce, half the
cream and half the butter in a saucepan
and bring to the boil. Remove from the
heat and add the remaining butter and
cream, stirring well. Strain.

Turn out the spinach mixture on to a
warm serving dish or 6 individual serving
plates, pour over the cream sauce and
serve immediately.

TARALLI WITH FENNEL

Serves 6

60 g/2 oz fresh yeast
500 g/1 lb 2 oz flour
2 tbsp fennel seeds
salt
120 g/4 oz lard, melted

Cream the yeast with a little lukewarm
water and set aside in a warm place to
activate when it will go frothy.

Mix together the flour, fennel seeds and
a pinch of salt in a large warmed bowl.
Make a well in the centre and pour in the
creamed yeast and melted lard. Mix

together well, then turn out on to a large
board and knead. Cover with oiled paper
and set aside in a warm place for about
2 hours to rise.

Knock back the dough and knead
again. Divide the dough in half and roll
each half out to the thickness of a pencil.
Twist these so that they resemble string
and then cut into 15-cm/6-inch lengths.
Make each into a ring. Arrange the taralli
on a floured cloth, cover with another
cloth and set aside in a warm place for
1½ hours until risen and quite soft.

Preheat the oven to 180° C/350° F, gas
mark 4.

Arrange the taralli on a baking sheet and
cook for 1 hour. They should have the
texture of biscuit on the inside.

PARMA FENNEL

Serves 6

1 tbsp butter
500 g/1 lb 2 oz fennel
salt
60 g/2 oz Parmesan cheese, grated

Preheat the oven to 230° C/450° F, gas
mark 8. Grease an ovenproof dish with the
butter.

Clean and trim the fennel, discarding the
heart. Cook in lightly salted boiling water
for about 10 minutes until *al dente*, still
firm. Remove, drain and set aside to cool.

Cut the fennel into fairly thick slices and
arrange a layer of fennel slices in the
bottom of the prepared dish. Sprinkle over
half the cheese and place another layer of
fennel on top. Continue layering until all
the fennel has been used, ending with a
sprinkling of cheese.

Bake in the oven for 8-10 minutes until
hot and the top is golden brown. Serve
immediately.

ROMAN BEANS WITH PORK FILLET

Serves 6

30 g/1 oz lard
1 tbsp minced onion
170 g/6 oz pork fillet, cut into small chunks
700 g/1½ lb broad beans, shelled
salt
freshly ground black pepper
3-4 tbsp water

Melt the lard in a large pan or flameproof
casserole. Add the onion and pork chunks
and cook for 5-7 minutes until the onion
is lightly coloured. Add the beans, season

with salt and pepper and stir in the water.

Increase the heat and cook for 15-20
minutes until the beans and pork are
cooked through and tender.

Turn the mixture on to a warm serving
dish and serve immediately.

SURPRISE PASTIES

Serves 6

250 g/8 oz cold leftover meat (see note below)
3 eggs, lightly beaten
2 tbsp Marsala or sweet white wine
350 g/12 oz frozen puff pastry, thawed

Preheat the oven to 220° C/425° F, gas
mark 7.

Finely chop the filling ingredients and
mix together in a bowl. Lightly beat
together 2 of the eggs with the Marsala or
wine. Stir the egg mixture into the filling
to bind.

Lightly knead the pastry and roll out on
a lightly floured board to 1 cm/½ inch
thick. Cut out 12 rounds with a 5-cm/
2-inch pastry cutter.

Dampen a baking sheet and arrange half
the pastry rounds on it. Lightly beat the
remaining egg. Spoon a little of the filling
into the centre of each pastry round and
brush the edge with beaten egg. Brush the
remaining rounds with the egg and place
on top of each filled round. Press together
firmly to seal and brush the tops with the
remaining beaten egg to glaze.

Bake in the oven for 10 minutes until
crisp and golden. Remove the pasties,
transfer to a warm serving dish and serve
immediately.

These pasties may be eaten cold, but they
taste better served hot.

Note: For the filling, use any leftovers you
have readily available. These might include
ham, cold roast chicken, beef, pork, or
lamb, mushrooms, eggs and even chicken
livers – hence the surprise!

Top: Surprise Pasties
Bottom: Parma Spinach Mould

MUTICOLOURED SALAD

Serves 6

200 g/7 oz radicchio
1 small curly endive
1 orange
1 tbsp finely sliced fennel
1 tsp mustard
2 tbsp oil
salt

Garnish:
1 orange, peeled, pith removed and thinly
  sliced
12 black olives, stoned and halved

Tear the radicchio and endive leaves into small pieces and place in a salad bowl.

Peel the orange very carefully, removing all the pith and membrane. Slice horizontally and remove all the pips. Add the orange and fennel to the salad bowl. Mix together the mustard and the oil and season with salt. Pour the mixture over the salad. (The acid in the orange will add the finishing touch to the dressing.)

Garnish with sliced oranges and halved, olives, if liked.

NEAPOLITAN CHRISTMAS EVE SALAD

Serves 6

1 cauliflower
salt
freshly ground black pepper
2 tbsp oil
1 tsp wine vinegar
6 anchovy fillets, rinsed
1-2 tbsp capers, rinsed
60 g/2 oz black olives, stoned

Cook the cauliflower in lightly salted boiling water for 7–8 minutes until *al dente*.

Drain the cauliflower, allow to cool slightly until you can handle it easily and then separate into florets. Arrange the florets in a serving bowl.

Mix together the oil and vinegar, season with salt and pepper and pour over the cauliflower.

Add the anchovies, capers and olives, mix well and serve.

Note: This salad is especially tasty with the addition of strong-flavoured flaked fish, such as smoked eel or smoked mackerel.

Top: Multicoloured Salad
Bottom: Neapolitan Christmas Eve Salad

DESSERTS

All Mediterranean peoples love sweet things – and Italians are no exception. There are many characteristic puddings and pastries to be found in Italy; some of them are prepared and eaten throughout the country, while others remain regional.

Pastries have, of course, become internationalized in recent years, and similar products may be found all over Italy, with only slight regional variations.

Italian ice cream is justifiably famous throughout the world for its richness, creaminess and immense variety of flavours. The finest ice cream is made only from cream, milk, eggs, sugar and fresh fruit. It is a brave cook, indeed, who would turn his or her hand to compete with the *gelateria* of Italy. Every major city boasts of its splendid ice cream parlours, but the best known are probably in Rome, where you can buy what is arguably the best ice cream in the world with a selection of more than 100 flavours!

A selection of other deliciously sweet confections follows, starting with the most characteristic and famous of Italian puddings – the ever popular Zabaglione.

ZABAGLIONE

Serves 4

6 egg yolks★
6 tbsp sugar
6 tbsp Marsala wine or sweet white wine

Put the egg yolks and sugar in a heatproof mixing bowl and set over a pan of hot, but not boiling water. Alternatively, place them in the top of a double boiler or *bain marie* and beat the mixture for 2-3 minutes. Gradually beat in the wine and continue beating until the mixture thickens and the whisk leaves a trail when lifted.

Pour the zabaglione into tall glasses and serve immediately while still warm.
★ Some recipes call for the use of the egg whites, as well as the yolks. This will result in a lighter, stiff mixture.

Top: Zabaglione with Peaches (see page 60)
Bottom: Raisin and Lemon Pancakes (see page 63)

Note: Marsala is a sweet Sicilian wine, which is often used in Italian cooking and which gives zabaglione its characteristic taste. However, if Marsala is not available, any sweet white dessert wine may be used as a substitute.

You can vary the basic recipe by adding several drops of a chosen liqueur, grated lemon or orange rind or a little vanilla essence.

ZABAGLIONE WITH PEACHES

Serves 6

3 tbsp sugar
6 tbsp water
6 ripe peaches, peeled, stoned and halved
12 glacé cherries
100 ml/3½ fl oz liqueur of your choice
1 plain sponge, Madeira or other plain cake
1 x zabaglione recipe quantity made with 1 egg
  yolk, 1tbsp sugar and 1 tbsp Marsala
  (see page 59)

Make a light syrup by dissolving the sugar in the water over low heat, stirring constantly. When the sugar has dissolved completely, simmer for 5 minutes. Add the peach halves and heat through.

Remove the peaches and place a glacé cherry in the cavity of each one.

Cut the cake in half horizontally, if necessary. Cut out 12 cake circles 5 cm/ 2 inches in diameter and arrange them on a serving dish.

Pour over the syrup and liqueur and place a peach half on each circle.

Prepare the zabaglione, pour over the fruit and serve. To add colour to the dish, finish off briefly under a hot grill.

Note: The peaches may also be sliced and for a quick and easy dessert, use canned peach halves or slices in fruit juice. The recipe may also be adapted for serving to children by omitting the liqueur and substituting peach nectar.

Summer Oranges (see page 62)

RUM DELIGHT

Serves 6

1 tbsp butter
6 tbsp caster sugar
5 eggs, separated
5 tbsp rum

Preheat the oven to 180° C/350° F, gas mark 4. Grease an ovenproof dish or a soufflé dish with the butter and sprinkle over 1 tsp of the sugar, turning the dish to coat the base.

Put the egg yolks in a mixing bowl with 5 tbsp of the remaining sugar and mix together thoroughly with a wooden spoon until the mixture becomes thick and creamy.

Beat the egg whites until they form stiff peaks.

Add half the rum to the egg yolk mixture and beat lightly. Carefully fold in the beaten egg whites.

Spoon the mixture into the prepared dish to form a mound. Smooth over the mound and, with the blade of a knife, make a cavity in the centre to allow the mixture to cook through.

Cook in the oven for 20 minutes. Briefly remove the dish from the oven, sprinkle over the remaining sugar and return to the oven for 5 minutes.

Pour the remaining rum into the cavity, ignite it and serve while still flaming.

SUMMER ORANGES

Serves 1

1 large orange
1 tbsp sugar
60 ml/2 fl oz orange liqueur
2 tbsp whipped cream
2 tbsp raspberry jam

Cut a thin disc off the top of the orange and reserve. Scoop out the flesh with a sharply pointed knife, taking care not to damage the skin.

Sprinkle the sugar and orange liqueur over the orange pulp and spoon it back into the skin, which now serves as a receptacle. Put a spoonful of whipped cream on top and cover with the disc. Chill in the refrigerator for 1 hour before serving.

Stir the remaining whipped cream into the jam and serve on the side, or serve the jam separately with the remaining cream piped on top.

Note: This is an excellent, light dessert to serve as part of a summer buffet lunch. It can be attractively displayed on the table and is easy to prepare in advance.

MARASCHINO PEARS

Serves 6

120 g/4 oz castor sugar
225 ml/8 fl oz water
225 ml/ 8 fl oz Maraschino liqueur
9 small to medium pears, peeled, halved and cored
1 orange, peeled and sliced
12 glacé plums

Dissolve the sugar in the water over low heat stirring constantly. When the sugar has dissolved completely, simmer for 5 minutes to make a light syrup. Stir in the Maraschino liqueur.

Add the pears and simmer gently for 10-15 minutes until just cooked through and tender.

Transfer the pears to 6 individual serving plates and garnish with the orange slices and plums.

TORRONE

Makes 700 g/1½ lb

200 g/7 oz honey
2 egg whites
200 g/7 oz sugar
400 g/14 oz almonds, coarsely ground
200 g/7 oz hazelnuts, coarsely ground
grated rind of 1 lemon
1 tbsp chopped crystallized or candied orange peel

Spread a sheet of rice paper to cover a pastry board.

Put the honey in a large heatproof bowl set over a pan of hot water or in the top of a double boiler or *bain marie*. Cook for 1½ hours, stirring with a wooden spoon, until the honey has formed a thick caramel.

Beat the egg whites until they form stiff peaks. Fold the egg white into the honey, very slowly and carefully, stirring constantly, so that the result is a thick white foam.

Place the sugar in a saucepan and melt over low heat. Increase the heat and cook to a caramel. Stir slowly and carefully, into the honey mixture.

Set the bowl containing the honey mixture over a pan of hot water, but not boiling water and continue to cook, stirring constantly; the thick liquid should become increasingly difficult to stir. Just before it caramelizes, add the almonds, hazelnuts, lemon rind and orange peel. Continue to mix thoroughly and quickly, as the mixture will now be hardening rapidly.

Below: Torrone

The torrone is ready as soon as you notice the characteristic aroma which the added fruit gives off.

Pour the torrone over the rice paper covered board and, with a spatula, spread it into a rectangle about 5 cm/2 inches deep. Place another sheet of rice paper on top and cover with a heavy weight. Leave for about 15 minutes.

Cut the torrone into large pieces and wrap in greaseproof paper to keep fresh.

Note: Preparing torrone is, admittedly, slow and laborious, but this festive dessert is so delicious it is well worth the effort.

RICOTTA CHEESECAKE

Serves 6

170 g/6 oz butter
225 g/8 oz flour
salt
4 egg yolks, lightly beaten
30 g/1 oz sugar
75 ml/2¹/₂ fl oz Marsala
1 egg white

Filling:
1 kg/2¹/₄ lb ricotta cheese
120 g/4 oz sugar
30 g/1 oz flour
grated rind of 1 lemon
grated rind of 1 orange
2 tbsp finely chopped glacé cherries
4 tbsp raisins
2 tbsp finely chopped almonds

Lightly grease a loose-bottomed cake tin with 2 tsp of the butter and set aside.

First make the pastry. Sift the flour and a pinch of salt into a mixing bowl. Make a well in the centre and add the remaining butter, egg yolks, sugar, Marsala and lemon rind. Combine all the ingredients thoroughly and knead lightly. Cover the dough and set aside in the refrigerator for 1 hour to rest.

Preheat the oven to 180° C/350° F, gas mark 4.

Remove the dough from the refrigerator and cut off about three-quarters. Roll it out into a thin circle and use to line the prepared cake tin. Set aside in the refrigerator while you make the filling.

Beat together the cheese, sugar, flour, lemon and orange rinds, glacé cherries and raisins until they are thoroughly mixed. Spoon the filling evenly into the pastry case and smooth the top. Sprinkle over the almonds.

Thinly roll out the remaining dough into a rectangle longer than the diameter of the cake tin. Cut it into narrow strips and arrange over the cheesecake filling to make a lattice pattern. Lightly beat the egg white and brush it over the lattice strips to glaze.

Bake in the oven for 1 hour until the pastry case is golden and the filling is firm. Remove the cake tin from the oven and place on a wire rack for 15 minutes to cool slightly. Remove from the tin and set aside to cool completely. Serve cold.

RAISIN AND LEMON PANCAKES

Serves 6

60 g/2 oz flour
salt
2 tsp sugar
1 egg
1 egg yolk
225 ml/8 fl oz milk
4 tbsp oil
1 tsp finely grated lemon rind
1 tbsp lemon juice

Filling:
2 tbsp sugar
juice of 1 lemon
6 tbsp raisins

Sift the flour and a pinch of salt into a mixing bowl and stir in the sugar. Add the egg, egg yolk, half the milk and 1 tsp oil and mix until smooth. Mix in the remaining milk, lemon rind and lemon juice and beat to form a light, airy batter the consistency of single cream. Strain, cover and set aside for 1 hour.

Meanwhile, make the filling. Dissolve the sugar in the lemon juice over low heat. Remove from the heat, add the raisins and set aside.

Heat 1 tsp of the remaining oil in a crêpe pan or heavy frying-pan until very hot. Pour in 2 tbsp of the batter and tilt so that it covers the bottom of the pan. Cook for 1-2 minutes, turn over with a spatula.

Transfer the pancake to a plate and keep warm while you cook the remainder, using more oil as required.

Reheat the filling and either fill the pancakes and roll them or fold in four and serve the lemon raisin mixture as a sauce.

Note: If you interleave the pancakes with greaseproof paper and you can keep them warm over a pan of hot water, but not boiling water without their becoming hard or rubbery.

CENCI

Makes about 24

120 g/4 oz flour
1¹/₂ tsp icing sugar
salt
1 egg
1 egg yolk
1 tbsp red wine
oil for deep-frying

Sift together the flour, ¹/₂ tsp of the icing sugar and a pinch of salt. Make a well in the centre and pour in the egg, egg yolk and wine. Gradually incorporate the flour into the liquid and mix until all the ingredients are thoroughly blended. Turn out the dough on to a lightly floured board and knead lightly. Cover and set aside in the refrigerator for 30 minutes-1 hour to rest.

Cut the dough into 2 equal pieces and roll out each piece on a lightly floured board until very thin. Cut into strips 12 mm/¹/₂ inch wide. Curl the strips round to make loose 'knots'.

Heat the oil in a deep-fryer to 190° C/375° F or until a cube of stale bread turns golden in 30 seconds.

Deep-fry the cenci, a few at a time, until puffed up and golden. Drain on absorbent paper and keep hot while you cook the remainder.

Transfer the cenci to a warm serving dish, sprinkle over the remaining icing sugar and serve immediately.

Note: Cenci may be eaten on their own as a delicious snack or served as an accompaniment to ice cream instead of wafers or langues du chat biscuits.

INDEX